Bonsai

*from native trees
and shrubs*

Creation • Cultivation • Care

Werner M. Busch

Bonsai
*from native trees
and shrubs*

David & Charles

A DAVID & CHARLES BOOK

First published in German as *Bonsai aus heimischen Bäumen und Sträuchern* by BLV Publishers Ltd, Munich Vienna Zurich

All photographs by Meyer-Horn except:
The German Bonsai Club 87
Busch 15, 16, 51tl, 55, 57, 61, 67, 78, 81, 88t, 91, 96tr, 101, 111, 124, 135bl, 135br, 141
Pall 10, 34, 37, 47, 108, 113, 114, 115
Schudde 2/3, 6/7, 8, 25l, 25r, 41, 42, 43, 46tl, 46tr, 46ml, 46mr, 46bl, 46bl, 46br, 65, 68, 73, 85, 92, 93, 100, 122, 135t, 140
Zachozky 88b
Stein 5, 13, 22, 83, 102, 109

p.1 Hornbeam
pp.2/3 Larch, created by W.D.Schudde
pp.6/7 Beech

Copyright © 1993, BLV Ltd, Munich
English translation © 1995
David & Charles publishers

Translator: Jenny Drey
Editor: Peter Davison
Gardening advisor: Jo Weeks

The publishers wish to thank Harry Tomlinson for reading and commenting on the proofs.

A catalogue record for this book is available from the British Library.

ISBN 0 7153 0336 8

Typeset by ABM Typographics Ltd, Hull
Printed and bound in Singapore by
C.S. Graphics Pte Ltd
for David & Charles
Brunel House   Newton Abbot   Devon

MAY 15 1996

Foreword

Twenty years ago, little was known in the West about bonsai. The first miniature tree forms were imported in large numbers from Japan; then came the so-called indoor bonsai, mainly from China. Today, bonsai are increasingly available commercially and now widely cultivated at home, with more and more native trees being grown in miniature.

This book is intended both as an introduction and as a source of reference. It is aimed at anyone who is interested in cultivating indigenous trees as bonsai – both beginners and experienced bonsai enthusiasts.

After a general introduction to the theory of bonsai cultivation and the techniques used to create traditional bonsai forms, it goes on to focus on native trees and their suitability for bonsai. It describes the peculiarities of each species, looking closely at cultivation methods and suggesting remedies to all common pests and diseases, thus serving as a useful basic text for the creation and cultivation of bonsai from native deciduous and coniferous trees.

The book is the result of ten years of professional experience growing bonsai from native trees. The experiences of other bonsai growers have also contributed a great deal to my work, and have been taken into account in the writing.

Some indigenous trees have not been covered, either due to lack of sufficient experience or because their short life expectancy makes them unsuitable as bonsai.

Contents

What is Bonsai?

Bonsai generally refers to the Chinese art of restricting the growth of trees through special cultivation techniques and keeping these miniature trees in tiny containers, giving them the look and power of expression of ancient trees despite their small size. The art of bonsai spread from China to Japan in the eleventh century, and we use the Japanese word *bonsai* to describe the art form as well as the trees themselves. The first miniature trees were introduced into Europe from Japan at the end of the nineteenth century and from there the technique spread to the United States.

In the Asian tradition, the parts of the tree that are particular features of age – strong roots, a thick trunk or powerful branches with a well-shaped crown of foliage – are emphasised and accentuated, often to extremes. With some Asian bonsai this led over the centuries to giant roots and excessively thick trunks, and often only a few branches.

Why bonsai?

If you think about it, it is obvious why these miniature trees excite so much interest, and not just in the East. Bonsai presents the opportunity to form a particularly close relationship with a tree; you can watch it and get to know it especially well. Bonsai growers understand their plant's needs so thoroughly – more than is possible with trees growing in the open – that they can predict its reaction to each change in cultivation methods and thus identify which method is most likely to help the plant develop and reveal its inner character in its outer form.

Bonsai critics often talk about the 'rape of nature', complaining that the trees are kept in pitiful conditions and given the tiniest amount of room, so they remain small. Anyone who believes this has neither had a good look at bonsai nor truly understands nature. Bonsai may be kept in small containers, but under optimum conditions – better conditions

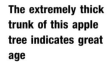
The extremely thick trunk of this apple tree indicates great age

than any plant could ever desire.

They are well looked after, watered and fed, the size of their branches and foliage is kept proportional to the size of their roots through constant pruning, and every branch is wired or trained into the best position for light.

A tree growing in the wild, perhaps in a crevice in the mountains in very restricted space, has a much more difficult time. It doesn't get much in the way of nutrients and receives water on a

very irregular basis. Branches that have grown too long quickly die off during dry periods. Poor conditions mean there is hardly any increase in growth above the ground as everything is invested in extending the root system. In heavily wooded situations individual trees are engaged in a constant battle for light. Repeated breaking of lower boughs by woodland creatures leads to dense regrowth, with the result that some branches do not get enough light and die off.

A tree chosen for bonsai does face a relatively demanding life but it is equipped by nature with the capability to adapt to differing conditions, so it does just that: it adapts. And thus begins a long-term relationship of mutual giving and receiving so often found in nature, as with the *Mycorrhiza* fungus, for example. It supplies the pine tree with active substances which make the pine more hardy; in return the tree feeds the fungus, so each profits from the other.

9

A bonsai is ideally positioned to get plenty of nutrients and water. It is protected from pests, looked after, and even its need to reproduce is catered for. It is allowed to grow to the limit of its potential and regular pruning to remove the parts the roots can no longer supply enable it to put forth new growth again.

Bonsai satisfy many of the needs of their human tenders: the need for responsibility, for creativity, for silent communication and the desire to work with nature and with others.

Bonsai as an art form

In China, miniature trees (*Penjing*), are described as 'silent poems' or 'living sculptures'. Bonsai are indeed created, in the way a sculptor shapes a piece of stone, but with one basic difference: the one is dead, the other is living.

As with any other art form, there is a great difference between simply dabbling with bonsai and creating a living work of art, and few will achieve a masterpiece. A Chinese professor of art once said, 'A master of bonsai must be three people in one: craftsman, gardener and artist. All three must be carefully trained.'

First familiarise yourself with the gardening aspect. Then develop the technical skills. Only then can you successfully shape the tree without harming it.

Creating bonsai

Bonsai is an interplay between creator and sculpture and growers never achieve their aims without

Right: An Arolla pine in its natural habitat. Trees like this, sculpted by nature, can be a fruitful source of ideas for bonsai cultivation

the help of the tree. The first shaping is a 'suggestion' to the tree to grow further in a particular direction. The tree's willingness to respond is gauged from its reaction to this first move. If the plant does not follow the suggestion, a new way must be found – a compromise. If it does respond, and extends its branches in the desired direction, the designer can intervene again and make further alterations to the growth habit.

The methods used by bonsai designers to persuade the tree to grow as they want it to often appear extreme. In some cases, branches are cut off in one place to get new growth in another direction, or branches are bent down using wires, to achieve the effect of an old tree. Most of these methods of cultivation have some equivalent in nature and so the plant is well able to cope. In the wild a tree will react to having its branches torn off (= pruning) by producing especially strong new shoots, and to a heavy burden of snow on its branches (= wiring downwards) by correcting its direction of growth. On rocky ground many trees have only a limited space into which they can extend their roots. In high mountain areas in particular, it is possible to find ancient trees that have remained dwarfed through lack of room for the roots to expand (= bonsai container).

The result of years of co-operation between person and plant is a compromise between the designer's original ideas and what the plant can contribute. Different designers have different ideas. One might try to keep the plant compact, thick, green and healthy and will be glad of many flowers and luxuriant fruit, expecting little more than that it should grow as

old as possible. Another will plan every branch of the plant exactly, aiming for a particular result and protecting the tree from anything that might jeopardise this. All bonsai growers must decide how much involvement they want in the tree's development and how much they leave to chance. This decision usually evolves over time spent with the bonsai.

The first attempts

Beginners should limit their early efforts to giving their plant harmonious proportions and a stable appearance. During the first few years they need plenty of helpful hints to achieve this. These take the form of rules that are

Left: European larch, formal upright form, height about 40cm (16in). *Designer: Burghard Stirnberg*

gradually internalised and only then consciously drawn on when particularly difficult cultivation problems need to be solved.

In order to understand a plant's natural, characteristic shape, you need to study the form of the tree in the wild. When you come to apply this form to the bonsai, the so-called bonsai styles can help (see p.26). Bonsai styles are a distillation of the most important elements of each of the different forms of growth found in nature. These elements are deliberately exaggerated, often to the very brink of what occurs naturally. The shape of the tree may be perfect, but it will only make a lasting impression on the observer if the various parts of its structure – bark, roots, trunk, branches and leaves – blend harmoniously. Harmonious blends can often be achieved by intuition. If you are not wholly confident, it is a good idea to apply the golden section rule, which is found time and again in nature. The golden section is a sequence of numbers in which every number derives from the sum of the two preceding numbers. Many shapes, both natural and man-made, may be traced back to the proportions of the golden section and we subconsciously see them as harmonious. Using the golden section helps determine the ideal relationship between, for example, the height of the trunk and the height of the tree as a whole. A 34cm (13in) high bonsai should have a bare trunk of 13cm (5in), with 21cm (8in) between the bottom branch and the top of the tree. The rule can be applied to most areas; it can serve to calculate the correct relationship between the thickness of the trunk and the height of the tree just as it

can be used for determining the size of gap between the branches.

No matter how well proportioned it looks, a bonsai only appears natural if it stands sturdily and believably. For example, an upright form looks more stable if the tip of the tree is arranged above the base of the roots, while with an inclined trunk form, the branches growing from the side opposite the direction of inclination are developed more strongly to provide balance. A cascade is given the appearance of stability by a short, strong branch growing upwards, counterbalancing the downwards growth of the trunk, and the tree is always planted in an especially deep container (see diagram left).

If you are close to achieving a well proportioned and sturdy-looking tree after the first

attempts at cultivation, you can extend your skills and try to make the tree more expressive. One way of doing this is by producing branches of a particular length and arrangement. Using repeated geometrical figures which combine to make a whole is a sure way of getting good results. In the case of conifers these figures are usually uneven triangles formed by the needles. The negative areas, the spaces between the individual branches, can also be used. A particularly expressive bonsai will fire your imagination and hold your interest through the composition made by the sum of its parts, the branches, leaves and negative areas. But before you can work on creative effects, you will have to practise caring for your tree and learn the techniques of cultivation.

Informal upright

Inclined trunk

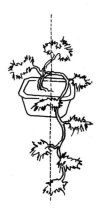

Cascade

Left: Although the normal ratio of 1:2 (trunk and foliage) is reversed, the tree appears balanced because the proportions are still correct. *Designer: Werner Trachsel*

Far left: This common beech in the informal upright style is about 40cm (16in) high. *Designer: Evi Streetz*

13

Cultivating bonsai

Situation

Plants use sunlight to manufacture oxygen and sugars from carbon dioxide (CO_2) and water, in a process called photosynthesis. The oxygen is expelled into the atmosphere, while the sugars, which serve as an energy reserve, are stored and used to maintain the plant's vital functions. As the plant utilizes the sugars, carbon dioxide is given off and oxygen is used. If a plant gets enough light it will manufacture more sugars during the day than it needs for maintaining its vital functions, enabling it to grow and its branches to thicken.

Every type of tree uses light differently and thus has a unique and individual need which should dictate its position when being grown as a bonsai. A sycamore, for example, needs a lot of light and therefore a sunny position to remain healthy, while a beech can only use small amounts of light and often thrives in the shade. Temperature also plays an important role. When it is very warm, the plant tries to cool down through evaporation via the leaf pores. As soon as the water reserves are exhausted, the leaf pores are closed to avoid losing any more, but when this happens photosynthesis stops because the oxygen needed for this is also absorbed through the leaf pores. Since the amount of water in a bonsai container is always limited there is usually no photosynthesis on hot days. On such days it is

Right: **Cold frame**

often sensible to move trees to an alternative shady place.

Native trees should be kept outside all year round, in the garden or on a balcony. If the weather is not too extreme, a carefully chosen spot under the open sky is ideal. Wind and rain harden the leaves making them more resistant to pests and diseases.

The role of the wind should not be underestimated. On a balcony, for instance, it prevents the build-up of heat during lengthy sunny periods. However, strong wind will dehydrate both the plant and the soil, so a compromise must be found between a corner out of the wind and a position in the open. The amount of wind particular species of tree can withstand is outlined under their individual descriptions.

Overwintering

The most sensitive part of any bonsai is the roots, which in most native trees begin to suffer in temperatures of below –5°C (23°F). To avoid the plant being damaged by frost, these trees are best taken out of their container in winter and planted in the garden. The tree should be planted at a depth so that the lowest branch just shows above the soil. The whole root system now has contact with the earth around it and the ground in winter is damp so it is usually not necessary to provide extra water, except in long dry periods. Choose a shady spot: strong sunlight during a heavy frost will evaporate the water in the branches and the frozen roots will be unable to rehydrate them.

It is not sensible to overwinter in a greenhouse unless you have a full air-conditioning system which ensures that the air temperature is kept constant. A disadvantage of overwintering indoors is that the plants often start to bud several weeks earlier than trees that have spent the winter in the open. As the days are still short there is a shortage of light which means that

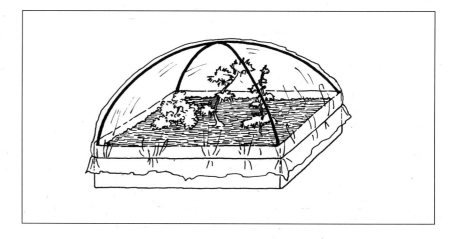

the leaves that are formed have long gaps between them.

If you have no garden, you can overwinter your plants on a balcony in a container – a vegetable crate is ideal – filled with a mixture of peat and sand. The container should be as large as possible. If there is a roof over the balcony which prevents rain from reaching the overwintering box, you will have to water it regularly. A light attic or a garage with windows are other suitable winter quarters. In these circumstances keep evergreens by the window and turn them every week. Again you will have to ensure that the plants have enough water, which can be tiresome if they are in the attic.

The tree can be prepared for winter once all the leaves have fallen. As soon as the buds start to swell in the spring, take the plant out of its winter quarters and prepare it for another year.

Watering

Watering must be carried out with greater than usual care. The container in which the bonsai is cultivated is much smaller than that of a normal pot plant, with the result that what water there is gets used up that much more quickly. With trees that are well rooted the major part of the water is used by the plant itself. Depending on the weather, however, a considerable amount may evaporate from the surface of the soil, which in bonsai containers is large in relation to volume. Mineral salts in the water, especially lime or calcium, remain in the container and may build up and lead to root damage. You can avoid this by using rainwater as often as you can. If this is not possible, always give enough water

to ensure that a large part of it runs away through the drainage holes in the bottom of the container, rinsing the soil of excess mineral salts. Of course you will also be washing away important nutrients and trace elements, so care must be taken with feeding. Trees have differing abilities to withstand salts in the soil; refer to the species guide for individual tolerances.

On hot days a lot of water evaporates from the leaves to cool the tree. Some salts are carried with the water into the leaves and deposited there, particularly in the cells at the leaves' edges. When the concentrations get too high it causes damage, turning the leaves brown at the edges. So whenever possible you should use water known to be low in mineral salts, especially on hot days.

There are no hard and fast rules on how often a plant should be watered, since the need for water varies greatly depending on the weather and the type of tree. Most water is used in hot sun or in strong wind. Whether it has rained or not, check the soil around the roots regularly as rain will run down the leaves of a tree with thick foliage, missing the container and leaving the soil dry. The soil surface is a good indicator: if it is only slightly damp or just dry, the bonsai needs watering.

Soil

A mixture of equal parts of peat, sand and loam (*Akadama*, an imported Japanese soil can be used instead of loam) makes a good growing medium for all the trees mentioned here. It is vital to remember that this mixture contains hardly any nutrients, and

In strong sunshine most of the water evaporates through the leaves in order to cool the tree, and a certain amount is also lost from the surface of the soil

Thick foliage directs rain over the edge of the container meaning that it must be watered even after heavy rain

Typical damage after hot weather

a good fertiliser is essential. The higher the level of loam in the mixture, the more fertiliser is needed. The species section deals with particular requirements for individual plants.

Features of different soil types

Far right: **A beech in autumn, grown from a wild seedling. It is about 50cm (20in) high**

Below: **In the proper setting, the sight of a bonsai cannot fail to impress the observer. A view of Pius Notter's bonsai garden**

• **Sand** makes the potting compost permeable. If there is a high proportion of sand, the surface dries out very quickly but underneath the soil will still be wet. This often means that the plant is watered again too soon, which is why sand is not used in large quantities.

• **Lava granules,** or perlag, can be used in part to replace sand in the growing medium. These are made from volcanic stone and are light and full of tiny holes which help to retain water. When not filled with water the holes take up air and thus help to provide the roots with oxygen. Lava contains many trace elements which the plant can use.

• **Peat** is used mainly because of its ability to retain water. It contains no nutrients, but is often prepared with lime and fertiliser. Humus can be used instead of peat. It retains water well and contains nutrients that are good for the plant and a high level of micro-organisms, which give the soil a loose, crumbly structure.

• **Loam** acts as a kind of buffer. It can hold high levels of water, without allowing the plant to stand in the wet, and slowly gives this water off again. Nutrients are also held and gradually released to the plant.

Soil with a high level of loam compacts very quickly and when dry it is rock hard. A granular loam soil from Japan called *Akadama* can be used instead of the usual loam in the soil mixture; in Japan it is often the only ingredient used for many trees. *Akadama* has a grainy texture which means that it does not compress quickly. It also has the positive features of loam – the pH value is neutral and the level of organic content and nutrients is very low.

Repotting

The best start for a young bonsai is to spend its first few years planted in the open garden. Every other year in spring it must be lifted and the roots growing directly beneath the trunk (the tap roots) must be removed so that only a ring of side roots remains. These roots, which will eventually form the main root system, now grow much stronger as they have to supply the needs of the whole tree. Over the next two years the tree will produce new roots and when it is next lifted some of these are cut away again, leaving only those necessary for the future root system. When the trunk has reached the right thickness, the tree can be lifted from the garden and planted into its first bonsai container.

If you do not have a garden, you can keep a young plant in a large container or a tub for a few years but you will need to change half the soil every two years. The roots should be treated as described above. The trunk of a container-grown tree is usually not as thick as that of one grown in the open, but there are certain advantages: container-grown bonsai are much easier to prune and shape from an early age.

A young tree needs new soil approximately every two years;

16

Cultivation

From top left to bottom right:

1 If the bonsai is pot-bound, use a knife to cut roots and free the root ball

2 Loosen the old soil with a hook

3 To encourage root growth, remove all the roots growing directly downwards

4 Cover the holes in the container with new mesh. Then add a thin drainage layer

5 Now put the tree back in the container. Add loam granules to half the height of the container. Lastly, add the bonsai soil mix

6 The roots growing around the base of the tree can be emphasised by placing the sand or loam granules around them. Any moss covering will also grow around rather than over these side roots

older bonsai can be repotted less frequently. The best time to repot all deciduous trees is in early spring before the first leaves appear; conifers may also be repotted at the end of summer. When repotting established bonsai you can remove a third of the roots and two thirds of the old soil. Leave the central root ball alone unless the root system has to be improved, in which case you may need to disturb it (see p.31). If not, then proceed as follows: use a hook to loosen the roots that are tightly packed together. The outer roots, which usually grow in circles around the container, will now hang down. Cut these to the length of the roots in the central ball. Partially remove the soil stuck between the remaining roots. Now

place the plant in the prepared container. You can put the tree directly on to the base of the container, so long as the root ball is big enough to lift the base of the trunk as high as the container rim.

The roots should not completely cover the drainage holes. Add the necessary drainage material from the side. If loam granules are used, fill up to half the height of container; if using other drainage material, such as gravel or perlag, fill to a third of the height of the container. Now fill to the rim with bonsai soil. Make sure that there are no spaces left between the roots by working the earth carefully between them using a stick. Finally, water in well. If the bonsai is going to be put in a particularly windy position, stabilize the root

system by tying in a wire running through the drainage holes. After repotting, protect the bonsai from the wind and sun for two weeks, and do not feed it.

Pruning

Regular pruning is one of the main methods by which a bonsai is kept small.

Depending on the stage of development, desired size, and type of tree, pruning is done in varying degrees and frequencies. A deciduous seedling is not pruned at all in its first year and only once in its second. Conifers are not pruned at all until their third year. If you want the trunk of a 3- to 5-year-old deciduous sapling to thicken quickly it should be cut back at most twice a year once the new growth has reached two thirds of the tree's planned height. This pruning can be hard, depending on the shape of the branches in the crown, and should leave only 1–5 leaves. If you want to have delicate branches and few visible cutting scars, and you are prepared to wait longer for the thickening of the trunk, then cut back the new growth only when between 5–8 leaves have appeared. Older, well-developed trees are pruned when the shoots have developed 5–8 leaves. The idiosyncrasies of different types of plants are dealt with under the individual species.

During normal growth a hormone is manufactured by the tips of the growing shoots and flows under the bast (soft inner bark), inhibiting the growth of buds lower down. When the top shoot is removed the hormone production stops, enabling the bud nearest the point of cutting to develop. This new bud now produces the inhibiting hormone so usually only one more bud will appear.

As long as the new shoots have already developed 1–3 leaves their tips are removed in late summer. This gives the shoots time to ripen and harden and to produce new buds to survive over winter. The process of removing the tips is called pinching out and is done with tweezers or your fingernails. If the supply of nitrates in the soil is not too high, the tree will now stop growing and prepare for the winter.

Removing large branches

After several years of cultivation it is often necessary to remove very large branches to aid or improve the plant's structure. This happens no matter how a bonsai is being

grown. With deciduous trees such radical pruning is best carried out during the peak leaf-growing period between mid-spring and early summer. During this time cut areas will grow over particularly fast. Concave or wen cutters are best for cutting off whole branches; both leave behind a concave wound which will heal more easily. Once the branch has been removed the wound should be treated with sealant. Particularly good results can be obtained with Japanese cut paste, which unlike some preparations is easily removed after the wound has healed.

Left: **Tools (clockwise from top): small and large wen cutters; broad and narrow concave branch cutters; special wire cutters for aluminium wire; Jin pliers which can also be used to bend stiff short ends of wire; tweezers to remove young shoots; root hook; wire brush to clean dead wood areas; bonsai brush to care for the surface of the soil; bending jacks to correct thick branches; shears to prune delicate and strong branches; leaf cutting scissors to remove leaves**

Far left: **Stronger branches are removed with wen or concave cutters and the scar is sealed**

Left: **Large cutting point after about six months**

Large branches on pines and spruces can be removed in winter as well as during the main growing season; larches, however, heal fastest in spring. With conifers you might also consider leaving the branch or a portion of it on the tree as a *jin* (see p.38).

Feeding

The first feed is given in spring when the shoots begin to show. This can be a fertiliser with a high nitrogen content as the need for nitrates is particularly high when growth begins. Deciduous trees need more nitrates than conifers. After the first feed, nutrients should be given weekly, fortnightly or monthly, depending on the weather and the type of fertiliser used – for instance, liquid fertilisers are easily washed away in heavy rain so will need to be given more regularly.

The nitrogen content of the fertiliser must be reduced as the year goes on, and by autumn the feed should contain no nitrates at all. To achieve this, different types of fertiliser are used throughout the feeding season. You might start the year with rapeseed pellets and finish feeding in August with cactus fertiliser, which has a particularly low nitrate content. There is a special potash/phosphate fertiliser which, if given in early autumn, encourages frost resistance and fattening. It is, however, difficult to get in liquid form and is only available from specialists in exact doses so if you are a beginner don't worry about using it. If you want to use only one sort of fertiliser you can get round this by giving the tree plenty during the growing season and gradually reducing the amount towards autumn.

Far right: **field maple in summer (see p.50)**

Chemical fertilisers

These contain nutrients that the plant can use immediately, and normally take the form of mineral salts in solution. As we have already noted, too high a mineral content in the soil can damage the plant. You should therefore be extremely careful with these fertilisers. To be on the safe side it is better to use only half the recommended concentration of fertiliser, but given relatively frequently. Before fertilising, make sure that the roots are nicely damp.

Both liquid mineral fertilisers and those in dry mixtures designated as specially for bonsai are suitable. Those available for amateur use are usually 'complete', which means they contain all the most important nutrients and sometimes also trace elements. The proportions in which the nutrients are present are given on the bottle so you know exactly what you are giving your bonsai.

Recently, so-called long-life fertilisers, which come in pellets or granules, have become widely available. The nutrient is contained in a material which weathers over time, gradually releasing the fertiliser. Be careful with these as well. Once they are in the soil you have no further control over the nutrients available to the plant.

Organic fertilisers

Here the nutrients are bound in an organic form and must be broken down by micro-organisms before the plant can use them. In a healthy soil the nutrients are continually released in small quantities and immediately taken up by the plant. There is therefore no danger of over-fertilising.

Most organic substances used as fertiliser contain nutrients in very unbalanced amounts. For example, hoof and horn and ground rapeseed contain a high level of nitrates and bonemeal contains a very high level of phosphates. Organic bonsai fertilisers are widely available, and usually consist of different organic elements in an appropriate mix for plants.

The properties and effects of plant nutrients

Nitrogen (N)

Pure nitrogen makes up about 78% of the earth's atmosphere. It is present in the plant as an element of chlorophyll and as a protein builder, and enables it to grow. In the soil nitrogen usually occurs in organic compounds. These are broken down by micro-organisms and the nitrogen can then be used by the plant. Plants take nitrogen through their roots; some, such as alder, can meet their needs for nitrogen from the air, with the help of so-called root nodule bacteria.

A lack of nitrogen is characterised by weak growth and pale yellow colouring in the leaves.

Phosphorus (P)

Phosphorus occurs naturally mainly in organic compounds such as protein and bones. Plants need phosphorus mainly for energy metabolism and other processes. They also use it to make nucleic acids and it promotes the development of flowers and fruit. Phosphorus is taken up through the roots and its availability depends largely on the pH value of the soil. Phosphorus is also absorbed by minerals present in clay, which can reduce its availability to the plant.

A lack of phosphorus is made

Right: **Spruce, about 70cm (28in) high, cultivated from a wild seedling.** *Designer: Werner Trachsel*

Particularly useful for the bonsai grower is its ability to promote frost resistance. Potassium is taken up through the roots and depending on its concentration can affect the amounts of usable calcium and magnesium available to the plant, so it is important that these elements are always present in balanced quantities in the soil. Organic fertilisers always contain elements of potassium. A selective potassium feed should be followed by a feed of mineral fertiliser.

A shortage of potassium can be recognised by brown or yellow edges to the leaves or entire leaves dying off.

Calcium (Ca), Lime
Calcium occurs in the soil in carbonate, sulphate or phosphate form, and forms part of many minerals and rocks. Its main use is to build the cell walls and it plays an important role in cell production and the growth of the roots. It is absorbed through the roots.

Fertilising with lime helps to neutralise an acid soil and has a beneficial effect on the structure of the soil, on the activity of micro-organisms and on the resulting availability of other nutrients. Hard water contains large amounts of calcium. Calcium deficiency is characterised by weak growth, a low resistance to illness or yellow shoots.

Magnesium (Mg)
Magnesium does not occur in pure form in nature and is found in the soil mainly as carbonate. Magnesium carbonate is the main constituent of common rocks such as dolomite, which makes up entire mountain ranges. It is vital for the development of chlorophyll in plants. It also plays a part in many metabolic processes.

apparent by the plant producing weak growth, despite having green leaves, and by a low resistance to illness and frost.

Potassium (K)
Potassium is a highly reactive element that forms part of many mineral compounds but does not occur in pure form in nature and is not found in organic compounds. It controls most metabolic procedures in plants and plays an important role because of its osmotic effect.

If a plant lacks magnesium its older leaves will turn yellow with the veins remaining green.

Sulphur (S)
Sulphur is a component of several amino acids. It is available in quantity in the air in the form of sulphur dioxide and is washed into the earth by rain so it can be ignored in fertilising.

Trace elements

Boron (B)
This is important for carbohydrate metabolism and the formation of cell walls.

Deficiency is indicated when young shoots turn yellow and die.

Copper (Cu)
Copper is a component of several enzymes, and takes part in protein synthesis.

A copper deficiency is visible by white tips to the leaves.

Manganese (Mn)
Manganese controls many metabolic processes.

If the plant is deficient in manganese, irregular brown spots will appear on the foliage. It is mostly the older leaves that are affected.

Zinc (Zn)
Zinc controls the activities of enzymes and the development of hormones. It also plays a part in photosynthesis.

Cobalt (Co)
Cobalt is needed by the rhizobins (nodule bacteria) for fixing nitrogen. (See alder p.58).

Molybdenum (Mo)
Molybdenum helps to control nitrogen metabolism. A deficiency is usually indicated by the yellowing and malformation of young leaves.

The natural rhythm of growth

The trees featured in this book exhibit secondary thickening, that is, the plants grow thicker as they get older. The cambium (see illustration) is a layer of cells between the bark and the wood. It develops wood cells inwards and bark cells outwards through cell division during the plant's growth period. The wood transports water from the roots to the far ends of the branches; part of the work of the bark cells, on the other hand, is to transport absorbed substances from the leaves to the tiniest root hairs. In spring the buds swell, mainly due to the rise in temperature, and deciduous trees begin to produce leaves, which are immediately capable of absorbing the substances necessary for growth. At this point the roots begin to grow and the new shoots continue to develop rapidly, finally hardening into branches. During the hardening phase the roots reach the peak of their growth, which finishes in midsummer with the onset of the second phase of leaf growth. A further phase of growth takes place with the hardening of the midsummer growth and another in autumn with the end of the fruit's development and the hardening of the last short burst of growth in preparation for winter. Conifers also exhibit a particularly strong root growth in late summer.

During the phases of strong root growth, absorption of nutrients is especially great. In autumn this serves to build up a reserve of nutrients which enables new shoots to grow in the spring. You can look at it the other way round: the roots that grow in autumn provide the plant with nutrients that are needed for developing the new growth in spring; the spring growth in turn provides the fast-growing roots with the nutrients that are necessary for midsummer growth.

Phases of particularly strong thickening occur between new spring growth and midsummer growth, and in autumn. Thickening in spring begins in order to develop new canals to transport the water supply to the new long-term growth and ends with the making of reserve cells; thickening in autumn is mainly due to the production of large reserves for next year's growth.

Through an understanding of the tree's growth rhythm comes the ability to make a number of useful decisions: the most favourable times for pruning the roots, for

Right: **Cross-section through wood, greatly simplified**

Centre: **The leaves on this lime tree have been cut back, which will significantly disrupt its natural growth patterns**

Far right: **This elm, shown in spring growth (see p.100), might be considered to be in twin-trunk style**

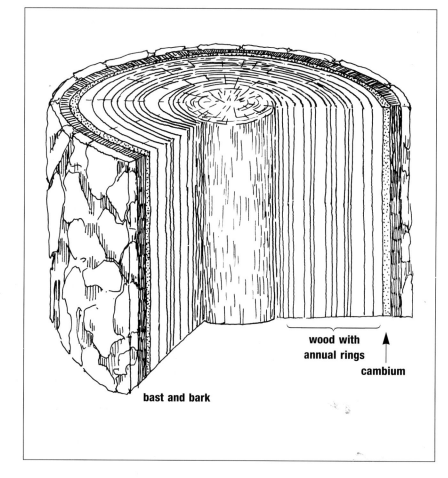

wood with annual rings

cambium

bast and bark

instance. With most deciduous trees it is easiest to prune the roots in spring, before the leaves appear. At that point they have built up enough reserves for new growth and will themselves start to develop again after the leaves appear. Pruning the roots early in autumn reduces the amount of reserves the tree can build up and therefore reduces the subsequent thickening growth with the result that the following spring the new shoots will be weaker.

The roots of conifers may be pruned as early as summer because they develop new roots particularly quickly during this period.

Bonsai growth patterns

In bonsai the natural pattern of growth described above can be influenced by various methods of cultivation and can be used to achieve specific results. Pruning while the shoots are still appearing in spring leads to a fast second burst of growth; some deciduous trees such as elm, lime, hornbeam and maple will even put forth a third and fourth burst if they are pruned early enough.

25

Bonsai styles

Japanese styles

Bonsai cultivation in Japan has a number of established styles (described below) that mimic the natural forms of trees in the wild. If we take this as a guideline then, strictly speaking, we ought to invent new styles for native western trees. In practice most of the Japanese styles can be used and adapted to suit western species. This is done by examining the habit of the tree in the wild, selecting the traditional style that is closest and modifying it to suit the species concerned. More detail is given in the individual species entries.

Far right: **This beech, in full summer leaf, is in informal upright style and is about 90cm (36in) high**

Broom

The trunk, as the tree's principal axis, does not go all the way to the top of the tree, but divides at a certain point into branches as equal as possible in length and weight. These grow in all directions, not just towards the observer. The foliage usually resembles an umbrella, and may be round, oval or domed. Conifers are not usually grown in the broom style.

Upright

In the upright style the difference between the front and back of the bonsai is distinct. From the front, the lower two thirds of the trunk should be easily visible and allow a view of the branches that grow out of the trunk, alternating between the left and the right sides. The lowest branch should be the thickest and subsequent branches should get thinner the further up the trunk they grow. The branches are usually arranged horizontally or gently drooping. When viewed from above all branches should be visible with no one branch growing directly above or below another.

Informal upright

The trunk has a bend which is often very pronounced, sometimes in an s-shape, and the branches are positioned as close to the outside of the bend in the trunk as possible. This form is suitable for most deciduous trees and conifers.

Formal upright

The trunk is very straight, usually as described above. Conifers are recommended for this style, but deciduous trees may also be used.

Twin-trunk

One root system supports a trunk that splits, producing two distinct trunks of differing size and thickness. The branches grow horizontally or gently drooping to accentuate the age of the tree. They are produced on alternate sides, first on the small trunk, then on the large trunk, from bottom to top. When viewed from the front there are no branches growing

directly between the two trunks. The branches at the bottom are thickest. In most cases the larger trunk stands straight, and the smaller leans outwards. Both trunks form a common crown.

Multiple-trunk

Several trees of differing sizes and thicknesses of trunk grow from one root system. The branches form a common crown and are usually horizontal.

Forest planting

Several single trees grow together in an often very shallow container. The group is arranged informally; the distance between the individual trees varies and they are not in a straight row. The smaller trees are on the edge of the group and the tallest and strongest tree is a third of the way in. The trees may either

have separate crowns or their foliage may be allowed to grow together.

Raft style

What appears to be several different trees are in fact branches growing upright from a horizontal trunk that is only partly visible above the soil. The 'trees' often make separate crowns.

Cascade

The trunk grows downwards, spilling over the edge of the container so that the tip of the tree is lower than the surface of the soil. This style is inspired by trees growing on mountainsides. Under constant pressure from storms and the weight of snow in their branches their main direction of growth is downwards. The trunk is either s-shaped or straight. From

the front, it resembles the upright style in shape. The branches, which become thinner the lower down they grow, are arranged horizontally on alternate sides of the trunk. Visual balance is achieved through the use of a high-sided container.

Windswept

This style, in which all living branches are growing in the same direction as if blown by the wind, can be applied to a broom or an upright form. It is particularly effective if the trunk is also leaning in the direction of the branches.

Literati

This form is characterised by a trunk which is particularly long and slender and may have a gentle curve. There are just a few branches, usually grouped at the top of the tree.

What makes a good bonsai?

A bonsai is always developing. To be truly successful it is important that all the individual elements of a tree – container, roots, trunk, branches, foliage and blossom – combine together to create a harmonious display.

Containers

It is vital that the size, shape and colour of the bonsai container is suitable for the tree. Pots should not be too dominant, nor too weak.

At the beginning of its development a bonsai will often be in a container that looks too big

and is not in an appropriate style, although as far as growth and cultivation goes it may be ideal. Once the designer decides that the tree is ready it will be transferred into a container that is suitable and appropriate for its subsequent cultivation and styling.

Over the course of the development of the bonsai, the ideal size, shape and colour of the pot may change several times. It is most likely to be the size of the pot that becomes unsuitable, and only rarely its shape or colour.

The following tips will help you choose a suitable container:

Size: Visual balance between the size of the tree and the pot is most easily achieved by ensuring that the diameter of the crown of the tree is the same as the diameter of the pot, and the depth of the pot corresponds roughly to the thickness of the base of the trunk.
Shape: Square or rectangular containers seldom suit delicate, round trees. A tree with a rounded crown will look best in an oval container.
Colour: The colours of the glaze on the pot should reflect some of the colours of the tree.

Soil surface

The surface of the soil requires care just as the tree does. Usually it is best to try to establish a complete covering of moss over it and there are several ways to achieve this. You can plant small pieces of moss and leave these to spread, or completely cover the surface with a single larger piece. Moss will develop more evenly if you use it in dried form, crumbled finely, and scatter the dust over the gently compacted surface of the soil. Keep the soil evenly moist with rainwater for a few weeks and a delicate and even covering of moss will develop.

The sort of moss suitable for the surface of bonsai containers is collected from sunny areas, not woodlands. Woodland moss requires a higher degree of humidity than is provided by the soil of a bonsai.

Stones can also be used to

From top left to bottom right:
1 Japanese and Chinese mass-produced containers
2 Hand-finished bonsai containers
3 Handmade porcelain containers are particularly popular for small bonsai
4 Old Chinese containers which are especially sought after

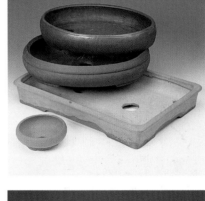

decorate the surface. They often serve to accentuate the age of the tree by making the trunk look shorter, so that its thickness is more apparent, and they fill the gaps between the roots.

Root systems

The surface roots, the strong roots that grow from the trunk and disappear into the earth, are especially effective if the roots are spread evenly in all directions. The

only direction they should not grow in is forwards, toward the observer. Trees that have been produced from cuttings often develop particularly good root bases because most of their roots grow from the cut and therefore lie on a level. Another way to attain good surface roots is to grow a young tree through a hole in a tile. When the trunk grows thicker than the hole in the tile, new roots develop on the top of the tile. They are all on one level and grow away in all directions.

Deciduous trees develop the strongest surface roots and these can be improved still further by removing all the roots that grow directly downwards from the trunk each time you repot them.

An existing root spread can nearly always be improved and corrected if necessary.

Grafting roots

If a strong root is broken or missing, you can graft a new one into the right place. Take a root of the required size from a tree of the same species, cut the top of the root into a wedge shape and slot it into a corresponding notch at the desired point on the trunk. Tie the graft together with raffia and cover it with a wound sealant.

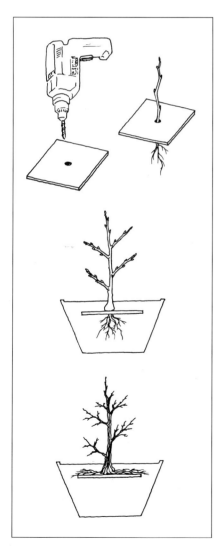

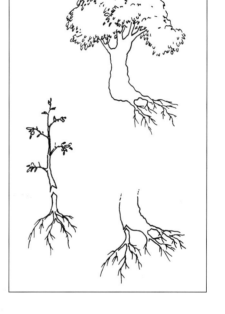

Encouraging root growth

A bonsai can be persuaded to develop a completely new root spread if its current one is not in the right place or if it is sparse. In spring remove a circular strip of bark, at least 1cm (½in) wide, from the area on the trunk where you want the new roots to grow; apply some rooting hormone to the spot and surround it with a potting compost that is low in nutrients.

Above left: The well-developed roots of a Norway maple

Above right: The roots of this hornbeam are not ideal, but they are capable of being developed by removing those that are too high and promoting the growth of surface roots

Left: Missing roots can be remedied by grafting

Far left: A strong and well-developed root spread can be achieved using a tile

31

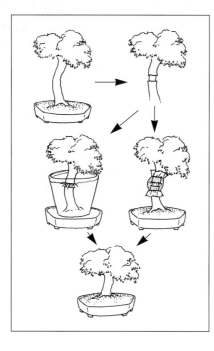

Above left: Creating a new root spread and shortening the trunk

Centre: By cutting back the roots at carefully chosen points you can create an even root spread

Below left: Fattening the base of the trunk using a taut wire to encourage the tree to develop a new root spread

Below centre and right: Single thick roots may be removed in the spring before the shoots appear so that the remaining ones can develop evenly

Far right: This hornbeam does not exhibit an ideal shape: the trunk is thicker where the first branch joins than it is below

After about a year enough new roots will usually have developed for the tree to be separated from its old ones.

Air-layering a new root spread

A similar effect to the tile method can be achieved in older specimens by tying a steel wire very tightly around the trunk at the point where you want a good root

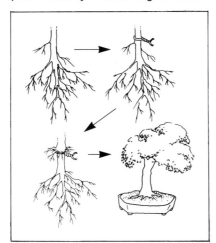

spread to develop and then surrounding the area with a potting compost that is low in nutrients. The hormones that encourage root growth formed in the shoots and in the foliage are carried downwards through the bark layer. They build up where the wire bites and ensure the development of the roots above it.

At first the roots are very thin but they develop particularly fast once the old roots have been removed as they are then the sole providers for the plant.

Selective root pruning

The root spread works particularly well if the individual roots are of

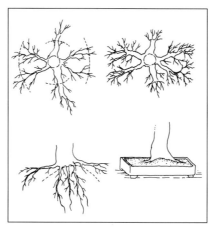

equal thickness. If one needs to be thickened, cut it back less strongly than the others. To prevent a root thickening too quickly cut it back hard.

Trunk

The perfect trunk starts from a thick, strong base and narrows gently to the top without any sudden changes in diameter. This ideal can be achieved if the trunk is pruned well several times in its first few years and the tip of the highest branch is thus encouraged to take over as the trunk.

The higher you allow the trunk to grow before you prune it, the more powerful it becomes but the pruning wounds become correspondingly bigger and the tree needs considerably more time to heal. Plants that are grown in the open for some time develop particularly sturdy trunks which accentuate their age; trees grown in containers from the start thicken through being given plenty of nourishment and only infrequent pruning of the leaves.

The length of the trunk from the roots to the first strong branch should not be too great and, to give the appearance of age, the

trunk should be short in comparison to its thickness. Proportions of 2:3 or 3:2 between trunk and crown are particularly harmonious. A trunk that is too long can be shortened by removing bark and encouraging secondary root growth (see p.31).

Most trees sooner or later develop a hard bark which will accentuate the trunk's character.

Branches

Branches should be significantly stronger and thicker where they are joined to the trunk, becoming narrower towards their ends where they develop finer and finer branches. On the trunk the lowest ones should be the thickest and the higher ones the thinnest. In the formal, upright style they must also grow on alternate sides of the trunk: left and right.

If a branch is too thin in proportion to the other branches, let it grow unrestrained without pruning while continuing to cut back the other branches regularly. This will encourage it to thicken and when it is as thick as you want it to be you can cut it back along with the other branches.

A branch that is too thick high up the tree should either be removed completely or cut back as soon as the shoots on it have two or three leaves. The other branches can be left to grow a bit stronger and then pruned later when they have caught up in strength.

A branch that has grown too thick will have to be removed. Don't cut it too close to begin with; leave a short section connected to the trunk. Within a short time a row of new buds will develop at the cutting point. Allow one of these buds to grow and form a thin branch and only then cut the rest of the old branch off as close to the trunk as possible, using wen- or concave branch-cutters. If the incision is well sealed, it will close up satisfactorily in all the trees described.

Where there are branches missing at significant points on the trunk they can be encouraged to form. A dormant bud at the right point can be started into growth in the spring before the new shoots appear by cutting the bark away to the wood across the trunk just above it. Within a short time the bud will grow to a branch, which can then be brought on to the appropriate thickness in the way described above.

Where no bud exists, a branch can be grafted on. There are several methods of doing this. The best way is to graft a seedling to the appropriate spot so that it grows into the tree. You will need to tie the seedling to the bonsai and cut into the wood of both plants at the point of contact. Another method is to drill a hole in the trunk and insert the seedling through the hole. In time the seedling will grow fatter than the hole and the cambium layers of both trees will join. Before removing the seedling's rootball ensure that the graft is complete by drying out the roots. If the leaves do not wilt then the seedling is receiving enough water from the bonsai trunk and its roots can be removed.

Alternatively, a bud from another tree can be grafted to the bonsai. The bud should have been cut in the winter and kept moist in the fridge. In spring a T-shaped cut is made in the bark of the bonsai as far as the cambium and the new bud is pushed into the T-shape, under the

bark. It is then tied in place with string and made airtight with a wound sealant. If the graft is successful, cultivate it with care and later follow the pruning methods described above. Unfortunately it is difficult to get branches like this to grow horizontally.

Leaves

The leaves of a bonsai should be as small as possible and proportionate to the tree, with a natural appearance. For this reason, species with naturally small leaves are preferred by bonsai growers. In any case the size of

Elements of Bonsai (header)

From above left to bottom right: A branch is added to a field maple

Left:
Another method for adding a branch to a bonsai

Far left: The trunk of this hornbeam tapers beautifully

35

the leaves decreases as the branches get smaller.

As long as the tree is planted out in the open, it will keep more or less to its natural leaf size. If it is pruned drastically at the same time as being planted in a container for the first time, it may grow particularly large leaves. With every subsequent pruning, the number of branches will multiply and with this increased branching, the leaves will get smaller.

Leaf cutting is an important method of improving branching and thereby making the leaves smaller. It involves the removal of part or all of the leaf during the period when the tree is producing new foliage. The leaf blades, ie all the green growth, must be removed, leaving only the stems. After a while the leaf buds in the stalk bases will develop into young shoots. Leaves that grow from these buds tend to be particularly small, but as many as possible must be encouraged to open at the same time to achieve good results. Most of the trees described will produce satisfactory results with only one leaf-cut a year, carried out at any time before midsummer. Some types of tree will take several leaf-cuts a year if they are healthy and well-fertilised (see individual descriptions).

One major disadvantage of leaf cutting is that it slows down thickening of the trunk and branches, as the new shoots use up some of the energy reserves that would otherwise be used for this purpose.

Flowers and fruit

Blossom and fruit should be considered in the overall design of the tree because of their decorative contribution. In bonsai they are usually about the same size as they would in the wild.

Trees that develop male and female blossom on the same plant are called monoecious; trees that produce male and female blossom on separate plants are dioecious. In dioecious plants, such as yew, only female plants will produce fruit.

All trees will flower as bonsai but, as in nature, they need to reach a certain age before doing so. Low nitrate fertiliser encourages the production of blossom. Some trees, such as the apple, bear more flowers if they are subjected to frost in winter.

Regular pruning can result in the removal of the flowering growth of the plant so if your bonsai does not flower and it is mature enough to do so, then it may be that it only develops its blossom on the previous year's wood. Some forest trees only produce large crops of flowers and fruit every few years.

Fruit can be left on the tree but it must then be given ample nutrients and it will almost always restrict the plant's rate of growth.

Sometimes an unhealthy tree may blossom particularly well. This emergency blossom is a sign that the tree needs attention. In these circumstances, all the options for treatment such as changing the soil, should be considered.

Right: **Field maple in autumn, height around 30cm (12in).** *Designer: Wolfgang Wirth*

Left: **This autumnal field maple is around 90cm (36in) high. Its large size makes its leaves seem smaller.**
Designer: Walter Pall

37

Shaping techniques

Pruning

Many deciduous trees can be shaped solely by careful pruning. To do this successfully it helps to know the growing habit of the type of tree you are pruning. If its leaves are arranged alternately, the last remaining bud on a branch after pruning will point in the direction that the new shoots will grow in. In some cases the next bud back will also grow at the same time and it is this that develops into a side branch while the first bud grows to form the tip of the cut branch. If the leaves are arranged symmetrically, such as in maple or ash, both buds at the cutting point will grow on, usually equally strongly. In this case, one should be directed upwards and the other encouraged to form a side branch by immediate follow-up pruning.

All branches growing directly downwards should be removed completely very early on; upward growing branches should be cut back hard.

Wiring

It is often quicker to get the shape you want by wiring. Existing branches that are not growing in the desired direction are wrapped in wire and then bent in the way you want them to grow. Aluminium wire is best, but because of its softness it needs to be relatively thick in order to exert sufficient pressure on the branch. This

thickness stops it cutting into the bark of the tree as quickly as thinner wire would. To wire thicker branches, copper or even steel wire is used. Plants that are still growing unrestrained in the garden cannot be wired as they thicken so quickly that wires usually become ingrown or at least leave marks.

The following rules are important in wiring:
• The wiring starts on the thicker branches and works up to the thinner ones.
• For additional stability two branches should be wired with each piece of wire wherever possible.
• The wires must be checked regularly, as many deciduous trees thicken in phases so the wire can very quickly and suddenly get too

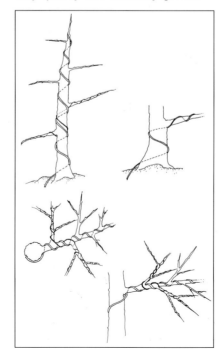

tight; in this case it should be removed at once before it leaves permanent scars.

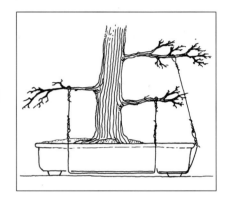

Anchoring

Branches that are several years old often cannot be wired without being damaged; they are better anchored. Anchoring works by pulling the appropriate branch into the right position with string or a thin wire. One end of the wire is secured to the branch which has been protected with a piece of tubing. The other end is either secured to a prepared point on the container or to a second branch, which should also be protected in the same way.

Working with dead wood (jin)

Dead branches or parts of the trunk with the bark stripped away can be incorporated into the design of a bonsai. Such features are common in nature: trees growing near the coast often have dead

Left: **This Scots pine, approximately 50cm (20in) high, has anchorage wires on its strong branches, training them without damaging the bark**

branches that are bleached brilliant white on the side facing into the wind and green branches bursting with health on the side sheltered from the wind.

If you aim to create this effect remember that the plants that exhibit the trait most frequently are conifers which are capable of shedding dead wood and staying healthy. Dead areas in deciduous trees are often attacked by fungus which can spread into the living tissue and kill the whole plant. So if you do decide to cultivate a deciduous tree like this you must watch the dead part carefully to ensure the disease does not spread to the rest of the tree.

Lime sulphur solution which lightens and preserves the wood can be applied to the stripped branches with a brush. This treatment should be repeated regularly; deciduous trees may need treating several times a year.

Selective fertilising

Since we know which nutrients the tree requires for which purpose, we can apply them selectively; for instance, to promote the thickening of the trunk of a young tree or to restrict growth of an old tree and to encourage it to develop blossom. Nutrients should be given proportionately to achieve this (see p.20).

39

The bonsai year

Midwinter

Often distinguished by particularly hard frosts. Deciduous trees (especially oaks) overwintering in open soil in the garden should be covered with a mulch of leaves or straw in temperatures below −10°C (14°F).

In mild winters trees can be sprayed to guard against the winter stages of various pests. Examine oaks for scale insects and apple trees for blood mites; after spraying they should be checked again. If you are overwintering the trees under glass, non-oil-based insecticides are generally more successful. Some pesticides only work above a certain minimum temperature.

Twigs to be used to make missing branches in spring (see p.35) can be cut now and stored somewhere cool and moist.

On frost-free days young seedlings and saplings can be taken from the wild (but only where permission has been obtained in advance!) They should be kept frost-free until spring.

Late winter

If you haven't already done so, spray against the overwintering stages of insect pests. The first shoots of the spindle tree appear now, if it has been overwintered free of frost. When the first tips of the leaves appear, spray them against mildew and then against other types of fungus.

Early spring

Alder, hazel and elm start to flower.

Most trees can be removed from their winter quarters and deciduous trees and larches can be cut back, leaving a part of the new growth on the tree.

All deciduous trees and conifers can be repotted. If necessary prune the roots and change the soil.

Trees that have branches missing can be given new ones using the methods described on page 35.

This is a good time to collect deciduous seedlings, and any young bonsai that you have been keeping in the open can now be planted in their first containers.

Unprotected spindle trees will now come into leaf. They should be sprayed immediately as described above.

Right: **This beech, shown in winter, is about 70cm (28in) high. It was cultivated from a sapling**

Mid spring

Almost all trees are now in leaf, with only oak, ash and beech not yet out. Late-developing trees that require new branches can be treated now (see p.35).

Most native trees will withstand late frosts up to −3°C (27°F). However, trees that have already put out shoots should be protected from lower temperatures. If necessary they can be taken inside overnight now and again. Oak, ash, walnut and spruce are particularly sensitive.

Depending on the stage of development (see individual species entries), the new shoots of deciduous trees can be cut back about 8–14 days after they appear.

Feeding can begin with a good basic fertiliser. Apple and pear trees should not be given too many nitrates, as otherwise the blossom or fruit might not appear. Try for particularly small leaves, but only on old and well-developed trees as the smaller the leaves, the more slowly the tree will develop.

Deciduous trees should be sprayed carefully against mildew and other harmful fungi with a fungicide as soon as the first tips of the leaves show. Treat greenfly on young spindle shoots with an environmentally-friendly pesticide; check larches for woodlice.

Hail is not uncommon now, and can badly damage the new shoots. Nets may be used to protect them.

Once they have put out their shoots, deciduous trees have a greatly increased need for water. Don't rely on rain as the foliage usually directs it over the sides of the container.

You can begin the styling of deciduous trees, larches and established pines, as the branches are now most receptive to forced change in direction of growth, and large pruning wounds will heal over quickly.

During this month maples, ash, sloe, hornbeam, larch, yew and some others blossom.

Late spring

Ash, oak and beech have now started producing shoots. Ash, oak and spruce are in particular danger from late frosts and need to be kept in a frost free place if temperatures below 0°C (32°F) are expected. When the tips of oak leaves appear they should be sprayed carefully against mildew; spray beeches against woolly aphid as soon as it appears using an environmentally-friendly spray. Lime, ash and elm should be examined and treated for leaf spot disease and spider mites.

Oak and beech can be pruned for the first time two weeks after shoots appear. After a further two weeks either reduce leaves that are too dense on beeches or leaf-cut; oaks should be leaf-cut. Leaf-cutting can also be carried out on lime, hornbeam, sycamore, chestnut and Norway maple. Larches and yews can be cut back, pines and junipers pinched back and the candles broken off pines. Some deciduous trees are now ready for a second pruning.

Left: **Beech in spring, shortly before coming into leaf**

Thorough feeding is now particularly important.

Keep an eye on wires, even newly applied ones, on fast-growing deciduous trees as they can quickly become in-grown.

Dwarf birch, apple and pear flower now, as do lime and oak.

Early summer

Most deciduous trees must now be pruned regularly. This often needs doing several times in quick succession on different parts of the tree because the individual shoots grow at different rates – usually the top third of the foliage first and then the rest.

Hot days are now more frequent so a reserve of rainwater should be collected, thus avoiding the problem of a build up of excess minerals in the soil. If new leaves develop brown edges they are either suffering from too high a level of lime in the earth or a lack of potash. Brown-leaf edges caused by fungus usually occur earlier. Potassium levels can now be increased in feeds for deciduous trees; apply a potassium-based mineral fertiliser in addition to rapeseed pellets or organic powder fertiliser. Make sure that the root ball is damp before giving the mineral fertiliser and check it one or two days later to ensure that it has not dried out.

Trees in their first year in a container can now be shaped. Juniper and larch can be pinched back further or even pruned if the new shoots have not yet been shortened and have started to become woody.

Thickening of the trunk and branches often begins suddenly, particularly in beeches, so make sure you examine wired

Right: **Beech in summer**

deciduous trees every two days and remove wires that have become too tight.

All deciduous trees and junipers should be checked regularly for red spider mite and greenfly which are on the rapid increase this month.

This is the last chance for leaf-cutting deciduous trees.

Cuttings can be taken from most deciduous trees.

Midsummer

Watering is the most important task this month. Rainwater is particularly beneficial to those deciduous trees that are sensitive to lime.

Pines can now be cut back.

Deciduous trees now grow irregularly. Reduce the nitrate level in their feed so they stop producing new shoots by end of the summer.

Keep a look out for red spider mites, now at their peak. Regular checks will help prevent blemishes on autumn leaves.

Check trees for mildew and treat if necessary.

Late summer

Feeds that are low in nitrogen should be used until autumn colour appears.

Pluck new shoots off deciduous trees.

Conifers can be repotted as they will quickly re-establish themselves. Protect them from strong sunshine for 14 days after they have been repotted. Conifer seedlings can be collected now. Get permission to dig them up if they are not on your land.

Water with rainwater as often as possible.

Check all trees for red spider mite and treat if necessary; deciduous trees should be examined for mildew and treated if necessary.

Early autumn

Seeds of most trees are now ripe and may be collected.

On hot days you should water well, but don't give any more feed.

Conifers can now be repotted and their roots pruned at the same time. Conifer seedlings can be dug up now, but only where permission has been obtained beforehand.

Mid autumn

As autumn colour is influenced by the level of nutrients in the soil, autumn colours in bonsai may occur at a different time to the same type of tree in the wild. (Ash and alder do not have autumn colours.) As the trees change colour, they may be given a final high-nitrogen feed; the nutrients are now stored and will ensure strong thickening growth next year. Autumn-fertilised plants will produce particularly large leaves in spring.

Deciduous trees that are to be overwintered under glass can cope with new soil and simultaneous root-pruning.

Late autumn

Put trees away for winter as soon as the first heavy frosts are forecast. Do not feed.

If you are overwintering deciduous trees under glass you can still change their soil and prune their roots.

Pines can also be wired.

Early winter

In temperatures below −5°C (23°F) trees should be further protected with covering.

Do not feed.

Pines that are overwintered frost-free can be wired.

Left: **Beech in autumn**

Starting a bonsai

There are several ways of creating a bonsai and the time each takes to work varies greatly. The method chosen really depends on personal considerations such as the age or patience of the cultivator. The different methods follow similar patterns and are generally applicable to most types of tree.

From seed

This is a very time-consuming method and needs experience, much patience and discipline. The result can be a particularly fine miniature tree, as cultivation methods applied to young trees leave no trace. The method is also kinder to the plant.

Seeds collected from different trees are treated differently in order to make them germinate. Those contained in berries should be removed from the flesh of the fruit (rowan), others can be sown straight away (birch, elm) and others have to be kept cool in damp sand (maple, hornbeam, beech, oak). A very few types can simply be stored in a dry place (pine, spruce) after collection.

The individual tree descriptions explain in more detail which method is used for which type of tree.

In its first year from seed, the seedling is not cut back. In the spring of the second year it should be planted in a separate container, and the main tap root removed. The seedling reacts to this by developing especially strong side roots. In the third year the branches are also pruned for the first time. As long as the trunk is still thin, the shoots are allowed to grow 10–20cm (4–8in) long before cutting back. The longer the shoots

Right: Lime saplings of one, two and five years old (with three years of cultivation outdoors)

Centre above and below: The roots of a one-year-old seedling can be reduced in the spring of the second year so that only the horizontal side roots remain

Far right: This small-leaved lime was planted outdoors for two years, developed into a bonsai at five years and has been kept in a container for the last three years

Bonsai

From above left to below right:
1 The bonsai-to-be is taken from the wild and the portion that will form the front view is decided upon
2 The plant is put in a temporary container
3 Anchoring points for the wiring are installed
4 The main branches are trained in the desired direction through wiring
5 Once the main branches are wired it becomes obvious which of the other branches need removing or shortening
6 These having been attended to, the tree should be left in a place protected from sun and wind until the first shoots appear

open as it can in a container. Under no circumstances should a tree growing in the open be wired, as thickening occurs much too quickly. Growth is often so vigorous that the tree has to be pruned at 3-weekly intervals during the growing season – particularly important if you plan to go away on holiday. Elms, for instance, if not pruned regularly, can lose delicately developed branches because their tips become too thick from strong uninhibited growth. The following rule should perhaps be considered: if a bonsai is to reach an eventual height of not more than 30cm (12in), it will develop fast enough in a container. Plants which you want to be taller can easily spend several years in the open. How fast a young plant develops in a pot depends very much on general care as well. Watering the plant according to its needs is important, as is providing sufficient fertiliser, the correct position, and a good growing medium.

From nursery stock

When you visit a nursery or garden centre, you will often find one or two plants that are suitable for bonsai cultivation. Unfortunately, apart from varieties for hedging, the stock of native trees in nurseries is not especially large. Specialist bonsai nurseries occasionally stock young native specimens. These are five- to ten-year old plants which have been cut back for several years and thereby prepared for cultivation as bonsai.

An advantage of using a nursery or garden centre plant for bonsai

are allowed to grow, the thicker the trunk and branches become.

Wherever a branch is pruned, a change in the direction of growth invariably follows. The structure of the branches is such that the gaps between the changes in direction get smaller and smaller from the

trunk to the tip of the branch; thus each new shoot should be cut back shorter than the previous one.

The tree will develop faster and stronger if it is planted in the open from its third year and pruned regularly, although it can seldom be designed so precisely in the cultivation is that, although it has to be paid for, you are getting a tree which has had a head-start in terms of strong growth. One possible disadvantage is that it may have already developed relatively thick branches which will have to be pruned, and occasionally even the trunk has to be cut back. The resulting wounds are large and take a long time to heal.

Apply the following principles to a nursery plant or young tree that is being chosen for bonsai cultivation: if the trunk has to be shortened a lot, the shape of the remaining length should fit the desired final form. The trunk should have branches from as far down as possible, and the root system should lie as much on a level as possible.

A nursery tree can be planted immediately into a temporary pot; it does not need to be kept in an open bed first as it should be strong enough already. Wooden boxes are ideal temporary containers. Plant the tree at such a depth that the roots remain clearly visible.

The method of shaping described below is only one of many. There are innumerable different possible shapes and the methods of cultivation are correspondingly varied.

After the tree has been planted in the box, select one side to become the front, using the root system, trunk and branches to help make the decision. Sometimes it is immediately obvious that some branches must be removed and this can be done straight away; or you can work systematically from the bottom to the top and will quickly recognise superfluous branches. Those remaining can be cut back to the right length and

the larger cuts sealed with a wound sealant. The branches are then trained in the desired position with the help of wires attached to nails inside the box. The part-trained bonsai can remain at least a year in the shaping container. Then the wires should be taken off, the tree put in a first bonsai pot and the branches can again be adjusted into the right position using wires.

From a wild sapling

It has already been pointed out that collecting a wild seedling is the oldest method of obtaining a plant for bonsai cultivation. But nowadays nature is so often spoilt by man's carelessness that this can only be justified in rare and exceptional cases. There are places in the wild where you may come across old trees, usually deciduous trees such as beech, oak or hornbeam, that have stayed small, possibly because they are growing near paths used by wildlife and so are regularly nibbled. Although they survive, they grow no taller, and

with increasing age their trunks and branches thicken.

In mountainous regions, where the growing season lasts only a few weeks, you will often find small and very strangely shaped conifers: larches, spruce or fir. Stunted by hostile conditions in their natural habitat, these trees are nevertheless often quite ancient.

Plants that may to us seem dwarfed fulfil important ecological functions both near wild animal paths and in mountainous regions. Some of these are particularly suitable for bonsai cultivation if by happy coincidence the root system, position of the branches and the size of the trunk have developed favourably.

Plants must never be taken from the wild without the permission of the relevant forest or national park authority.

Sometimes digging up trees can save them from inevitable destruction, where for example they might be growing on a building site waiting to be mown down by a bulldozer, or simply have been uprooted in a storm. If you want to collect a tree from the wild bear in mind the following points necessary for their survival:

Left: **Beech in autumn, height around 70cm (28in), cultivated from a wild sapling.** *Designer: Walter Pall*

Bonsai

Buds of native trees and shrubs (from left to right): Sweet chestnut, common oak and durmast oak, Norway maple, field maple, sycamore, small-leaved lime

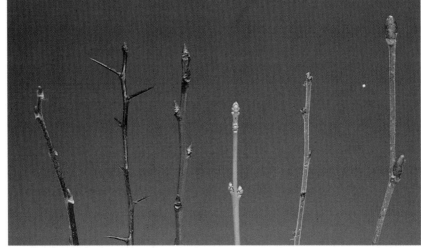

Willow, hawthorn, blackthorn, spindle, Arctic birch, hazelnut

Smooth-leaved elm, pear, apple, silver birch, black alder, hornbeam, ash, rowan, walnut

Far right: **Hornbeam, height around 90cm (3ft), grown from a rough bonsai**

1 Most deciduous trees can only be gathered successfully in the early spring, just before the first shoots appear.
2 Make sure that as many roots are left on the plant as possible. Plants growing between rocks should really be left.
3 As you will have 'pruned' the roots by digging up the tree, you should prune the branches back at the same time.
4 After removal, allow the tree to regenerate itself in a partially shaded place in the open or in a bigger plant container for 1–2 years.

Trees taken from the wild are often decades old, indicated by the amount of bark. By digging up such a tree you take on a great responsibility and any alterations to the shape, apart from through pruning, should be carried out very carefully. You should be especially careful not to damage the bark, which is a valuable design element. In Japan, trees such as these are left for many years to get used to their surroundings. The only shaping during this period of rest is regular pruning.

Which trees are suitable for bonsai?

More or less any tree can be grown in miniature form in a bonsai container. But this in itself does not mean that it is a bonsai. A bonsai is a cultivated miniature tree. This implies the use of special techniques to create a particular tree form with as much power of expression as possible and is only achieved through the joint effort of the tree and the cultivator. A tree must lend itself to bonsai cultivation: simply being a tree is not enough. It must fulfil the following criteria: the whole plant and its individual branches should be capable of living for at least 50 years. The leaves should not be greater than a certain size or should at least be in a reasonable proportion to the size of the tree. The tree should be able to stand constant pruning and react to it by putting forth new growth. The branches should be able to grow into a delicate filigree network. The restricted size of a bonsai container means the tree must be able to tolerate sudden changes in the soil moisture and temperature. Although not all the varieties of tree which follow are ideally suited for bonsai cultivation, all will at least produce satisfactory results if you make careful and consistent use of the described bonsai techniques.

Field maple

(Acer campestre)

Most of us know the field maple as a hedging plant and as it is rather unobtrusive in the wild it is often overlooked. When it is allowed to grow as an individual plant, it eventually produces a short trunk and a round crown. It has umbels of inconspicuous androgynous or unisexual flowers in late spring. After insect pollination the flowers develop into pairs of little winged nuts. These ripen in late summer and are spread by the wind.

The relatively small leaves, 3–5cm (1¼–2in) long, are arranged symmetrically and grow in groups of 3 to 5. They appear shortly before or with the blossom and turn bright yellow to orange in autumn.

The branches often have corky strips of bark along them. The bark on the trunk starts off smooth and later becomes tough and deeply patterned.

In the wild the field maple grows along with a mixture of other tree species, mainly oak and hornbeam, and it is often found on the edge of woods.

As bonsai

The field maple bonsai likes a sunny or partially shady site and is able to survive in windy situations. It can be given hard tap water and tolerates slightly higher levels of lime in the soil so can survive long dry, sunny periods, usually without any damage to its leaves. But it must be in a position to receive rainwater whenever possible.

A mixture of loam granules, sand and peat, in proportions of 2:1:1 provides a suitable growing medium. Fertilise from late spring to midsummer with organic bonsai fertiliser and prepare for autumn with a low-nitrate fertiliser that is rich in potassium. It can be overwintered planted out in a shady place in the garden or on a balcony in a box filled with sand and peat. Repot every 2 years.

Shaping

Of the Japanese forms, the broom style comes nearest to the natural habit of the field maple; the formal upright style is also suitable. Other styles are also quite acceptable.

The tree has a stiff and gawky way of growing and it is this that presents the most problems and necessitates particularly consistent basic cultivation.

Pruning

Seedlings and specimens from the wild can be pruned as described for the sycamore (see p.52). If the plant has already been shaped, all the branches should be cut back before the new shoots appear in the spring to allow for the current year's growth. Where two branches are blocking each other's growth one must be removed. Once this first pruning of the year is over, every remaining bud should have sufficient space for the new shoots to form a green canopy, with no gaps.

Depending on the stage of development of the tree, the spring shoots may be pruned earlier or later. If the trunk and the branches still have to thicken, wait until the shoots are at least 20cm (8in) long, and then cut back to 1–3 pairs of leaves.

If you prefer more delicate branches to a thick trunk, then the first shoots can be pruned back to 1 or 2 pairs of leaves when they reach a length of about 10cm (4in). After every pruning the field maple will recover enough to produce new growth within 2–3 weeks so the last pruning should be done in midsummer. After this the shoots are nipped back, which usually succeeds in stopping new shoots from growing. Leaf-cutting in early summer can make the leaves smaller and the branches more delicate, but it will hinder thickening.

In order to prevent too many flowers being produced, thicker branches should be removed either at the end of winter or after the leaves have appeared in spring. Larger wounds heal more quickly if they are treated with a wound sealant, which also protects against infection.

Usually a lot of buds grow around a large wound. It is a good idea to remove these early and leave only those that you want to develop into a new branch.

Wiring

As with all types of maple, the bark of the field maple is very sensitive, and wiring must be carried out very carefully. Wires that are too tight often leave permanent scars. To prevent in-growing, check the wires regularly.

Branches up to a year old are usually easy to bend. When shaping older branches, use tension wires.

Propagation

Collect seeds from late summer on, keep them in damp sand in the fridge and sow them in spring. Young plants between 2 and 4 years old and cultivated bonsai are available in specialist bonsai nurseries.

More recently, a particularly small-leaved variety (*A. campestre* 'Nana') and a red-leaved variation (*A. campestre* 'Purpurea') have also been available.

Nature seldom provides perfect specimens. However, old hedge plants can sometimes be trained into bonsai.

51

Sycamore and Norway maple

(Acer pseudoplatanus/Acer platanoides)

These two species are featured together as they look very similar when cultivated as bonsai and their needs are also similar. The few ways in which they do differ are clearly explained.

Both grow to 25m (80ft) high in the wild and both have a short trunk and a domed crown. While the bark of the sycamore falls away in flat, relatively small flakes, that of the Norway maple develops vertical fissures. The small flowers are polygamous and are borne in umbels. In the sycamore they appear after the leaves; in the Norway maple they are produced before or with the leaves and are bright yellow. Both are pollinated by insects and produce little winged fruit, which are spread by the wind. The leaves usually have 5 lobes, with particularly pointed edges in the Norway maple, and are arranged symmetrically as with all types of maple. They appear in mid-spring, and in autumn those of the sycamore become a bright yellow, while those of the Norway maple colour from orange to red.

As bonsai

Both species thrive in a sunny or partially shaded site, but the sycamore reacts to excessive heat by dropping some of its leaves. Both tolerate a windy situation, but under these conditions they will need plenty of water and should be watered several times a day in extreme weather. They like lime and can stand a slightly higher pH level in the soil so can safely be given hard tap water.

The most suitable potting compost is equal amounts, in weight, of Japanese loam granules, sand and peat (1:1:1). Every 2 years the soil should be changed and at the same time the roots should be pruned. Feed with organic bonsai fertiliser from when new shoots appear until the end of summer. A liquid mineral fertiliser will achieve good results.

Norway maple and sycamore are both very hardy, but should be overwintered either planted out in the garden among other trees to protect them from extreme cold and for the roots to stay evenly damp, or on a balcony in a box filled with peat and sand.

Shaping

Of the Japanese styles, the broom is the closest to their natural shape. The formal upright style produces a leaf canopy with a rounded crown, so it is also suitable. You can, of course, consider other forms as well. The leaves are relatively large so the eventual height of the tree should not be less than 50cm (20in).

Pruning

A sapling is pruned for the first time in its second year and the height of the future bonsai trunk is usually established at this point. If you want the tree to be about 75cm (30in) high you should prune the young tree in early summer to a height of 25cm (10in), just above a node. In a short time 2 new shoots will develop near the cut. One of these can be trained into an extension of the trunk, and the other into the first branch through further pruning after it has grown 3 pairs of leaves.

In spring of the following year, the trunk extension is cut back before the new spring growth appears. Ideally, the distance between the first side branch and cutting point should be a little shorter than the length of the trunk from roots to the first branch.

Two new shoots will grow in the axils of the 2 highest leaves and again one will form the trunk extension, and the other, through careful pruning, the second side branch. The third side branch can be created in the same way in early summer of the same year.

If you want to cultivate a garden centre plant or a wild seedling, a

Far right: **Sycamore in autumn colours, height around 60cm (2ft), 12 years old, cultivated from a part-prepared plant**

Below: **Leaf of the Norway maple (left) and of sycamore (right)**

first good pruning is best carried out in spring before the shoots appear. At the same time you should prune the roots, which will prevent bleeding from the wounds. Maple species will often bleed after cutting back in early spring. This usually stops of its own accord after a few days.

After the first hard pruning in spring, an untrained tree or hedge plant will need to be cut back again when the shoots have about 3 pairs of leaves towards the top of the tree and about 7 pairs of leaves in the lower branches. The longer a shoot is allowed to grow, the stronger and thicker it will ultimately become. About 2 to 4 weeks later, a new shoot will appear and this should be cut back in order to make the tree produce a third flush of growth, which is nipped back after the first or second pair of leaves appear.

If the tree has already been shaped, all the buds at the tips of the shoots are removed before the new spring growth starts, to encourage side shoots. The shoots that then follow are cut back from a length of 3 pairs of leaves to 1 or 2. Often there will be no further shoots, and the remaining leaves

continue to grow instead.

At the end of spring leaf-cutting can be carried out on a healthy tree, stimulating growth that has come to a halt, and contributing to the development of smaller leaves and more delicate branches. Longer shoots will now appear, particularly in the top third of the leaf canopy. These must be cut back once they have produced three leaf pairs or nipped out sooner.

Any large cuts that the tree suffers between the start of the growth period and the end of spring will grow over quickly and cause no damage if they are sealed well.

Wiring

Both species can be cultivated without wire if they are prepared for bonsai from seedlings. If you need to pull an older rough tree into shape, you will have to resort to wire. Young branches up to 2 years old are easy to bend but older branches are better pulled into shape because they are already hard, and you must be careful that the wires do not leave any unwanted scars in the bark.

Propagation

Seeds are collected in early autumn, kept in damp sand in the fridge, and sown in the spring. Plants of 1 or 2 years old are often found at the edges of cemeteries, in parks or in your own garden. Older raw material can sometimes be found here too.

Young plants and ready-trained trees are seldom available in bonsai nurseries.

Montpelier maple

(Acer monspessulanum)

The Montpelier maple, which grows as a small tree or large shrub, is not very common or well-known in Northern Europe. It prefers warmer climes and lime-rich soil. The dark green leaves appear at the same time as the flowers and turn yellow in autumn. The flowers are produced in umbels and pollinated by insects to form the typical maple seeds – two winged nuts grown together – and are spread by the wind. The bark which is smooth at first becomes easily torn and flaky when old.

As bonsai

The Montpelier maple prefers a sunny position as a bonsai and can be kept relatively dry. It is very sensitive to constantly wet soil, but tolerates tap water well. The most suitable growing medium is a mixture of loam granules and fine gravel in proportions of 5:1 in weight, which is renewed every 2 to 3 years. The roots are cut back at the same time.

The Montpelier maple requires little feeding, as it grows very slowly. From the appearance of the first shoots until late summer a solid organic fertiliser can be given every 2 weeks.

Leaf-cutting is not really necessary because the leaves are already small but it may be done to stimulate growth, which otherwise stops early in the year, and thereby make the tree develop faster.

It is not especially hardy in the winter, but can still be planted out in the garden with no problems. In temperatures below −5°C (23°F) it should be given a protective covering of straw, leaves or twigs.

Shaping

All the Japanese forms are suitable. It will grow almost of its own accord in the broom style. Regular pruning is all that is needed for this to happen.

Pruning

A. monspessulanum seedlings are not cut back in the first 2 years. In spring of the third year the trunk is cut down to the desired height. Older raw material may be shaped between the swelling of the buds in spring and the end of summer. If no leaves have grown by the time

Right: **Montpelier maple in summer, height around 25cm (10in), age about 8 years, cultivated from a young plant**

training starts, the roots should be pruned well at the same time. Growth is slow, so with plants that have already been shaped new growth is reduced by half only once a year at the end of spring. Unlike other types of maple, the Montpelier will not re-sprout after this without help in the form of a good feeding during the production of the spring shoots.

Wiring

Very thin branches of 1 or 2 years old can easily be wired. Despite the fact that the Montpelier maple produces only modest thickening, the wires should still be checked regularly to avoid pressure points.

The bark on older branches can be protected from permanent scars by anchoring rather than wiring.

Propagation

Ripe seeds are kept in damp sand in the fridge over the winter and sown in the spring. Young plants and older cultivated bonsai can be bought from some bonsai nurseries. Natural seedlings suitable for bonsai are uncommon and should not be taken from the wild because the plants are rare.

Pests

Leaf mites like to attack young shoots, whose leaves then roll up and do not fully develop. A non-toxic anti-leaf-mite pesticide is used to control them.

Various gall mites cause a spotty, felt-like covering. Several generations of these live among the leaf hairs which become larger due to their sucking, and which may turn browny-red. The eggs overwinter in little gaps and cracks in the bark. They need to be controlled for visual reasons, perhaps a forthcoming exhibition. The infestation can be reduced by removing the affected leaves. A bad infestation is treated with a mite spray. One type of gall mite causes longish, pointed red galls a few millimetres in size to develop on the tops of the leaves. Remove and destroy the affected leaves to control them.

The rose cicada (*Thyphlocyba rosae*) and its larvae cause light specks on the leaves. The affected leaves usually die so a bad infestation should be treated with an environmentally-friendly anti-sucking insect pesticide.

Fungal diseases

Mildew is characterised by a whitish grey covering on the top of the leaf. This harmful fungus can occur at any time during the leaf-producing period and overwinters on dropped leaves. It can be controlled by feeding with a low-nitrate fertiliser and spraying with a mildew fungicide in spring when the leaves appear. Another fungus, *Rhytisma acerinum*, causes tar spot disease, which is recognised by yellowish spots, which later turn black, on the edges of the leaves. Treat in spring with a fungicide containing copper.

Red spot fungus (*Nectria cinnabarina*) is apparent through partial or complete dying off of branches and orangey-red spots developing on the dead wood. The fungus infests the plant through fresh cuts or recently dead parts of the plant. It grows back from the cut or dead wood into the living tree, and kills it. Control it by cutting back to the healthy wood, and treat cuts with a fungicidal wound sealant.

Left: An attack of gall mites on a sycamore

Left: Mildew on a field maple

57

Common alder and grey alder

(Alnus glutinosa/Alnus incana)

The trunk of the common alder produces horizontal branches from the ground to the top of the tree; it is one of the few deciduous trees that forms the conical silhouette that is typical of a conifer. The grey alder grows more thickly and irregularly.

The flowers are formed in the summer of the previous year and appear from early to mid-spring. In common alder the male catkins are brown, in grey alder they are yellow. The inconspicuous female flowers are wind pollinated. The seed, little nuts 2–4mm ($\frac{1}{16}$–$\frac{1}{8}$in) in size, develop in a small cone and ripen from early to mid-autumn.

The alternate leaves, widely ovate in common alder and pointed ovate in grey alder, appear after flowering. They do not change colour in autumn, but fall while still green, after the first frost if not before.

The brown-black bark of the common alder develops a flat, cork-like surface with age. The bark of the grey alder is smooth and grey.

Micro-organisms found in the root nodules bind nitrogen from the air and supply it to the tree.

The common alder is found on the banks of streams and rivers, including flood areas, and in marsh and meadow woodlands. The grey alder is often found near running water in mountainous regions.

As bonsai

Common alder grows quickly and is tolerant of pruning so it is an excellent candidate for training as bonsai; it is to be preferred over grey alder because of the latter's extremely short life expectancy. Common alder likes a sunny or part-shaded position but should be protected from strong wind.

Alders need a lot of water. You can save yourself a great deal of effort by putting them in the shade during hot weather. Common alder should be given as much rain or softened water as possible. It cannot tolerate large amounts of

lime in the soil, so must be watered constantly to wash away the deposits. Grey alder may be watered with hard tap water. It also tolerates a somewhat higher soil pH. To achieve a thick trunk quickly alders are best planted in the open in their first year; a more delicate network of branches will develop only after the tree is placed in a bonsai container.

Common alder has no particular soil requirements and you can get good results from a combination of peat, sand and loam granules (Akadama) in proportions of 2:1:1. Grey alder must not be planted in acidic mixtures.

Fertilise with solid organic bonsai fertiliser from mid-spring to late summer.

Overwinter the plants in a shady place in the garden. Remove the rootball from its pot and plant in the earth. They may also be overwintered on a balcony in a box filled with peat and sand.

Shaping

Training should not begin while the tree is still small since the leaves can only be reduced in size after several years of cultivation in a pot and will look too large on a young plant.

The formal upright style is the nearest Japanese form to the tree's natural habit; other styles are also possible.

The common alder dries out very quickly with the result that one or two branches may well die off. A new shoot often grows underneath the dead branch so these lost branches are relatively easy to replace. If this does happen, cut back the new shoot only occasionally until it has reached the thickness of the

branch it is replacing. Young plants are best shaped from mid-spring to early summer. Plants shaped in the winter are unable to seal large wounds easily and should be kept frost free.

Pruning

Saplings are cut back by half in early summer of the second year. Later shoots are cut back to 1–3 leaves and to a length of about half of the planned total height of the tree, depending on the position of the branch in the tree.

If alders are in the open and not

repotted annually they should be cut back up to 5 times a year, depending on the weather, to avoid having to make cuts that are too large. Plants kept in containers in partial shade and constant damp will grow strongly. Otherwise do not expect more than three new shoots a year.

With plants that have already been shaped, allow the first spring growth to reach a length of about 20cm (8in) before it is cut back. Shoots that are produced later can be cut back sooner

Leaf-cutting encourages branching and is well tolerated by the tree. It can be done about

Right: **The ripe cones with small fruit (above) and the cones and catkins for the following year are all present on the same branch in autumn. The common alder (below) is distinguished from the grey alder by the flattened tips of its leaves**

every four weeks after the first shoots have appeared and may sometimes reduce the size of the leaves, but only rarely.

Thicker branches should only be pruned during the growing season (spring–summer), because cuts made in autumn and winter do not heal well.

Wiring

Only wire alders during the growing season, either in spring or after the first pruning. Young branches stay elastic for a long time so are easily wired. Check the wires constantly to prevent in-growing, as thickening often occurs in spurts.

Older branches are best tensioned in spring as the first shoots appear. They will then keep to the desired direction in winter.

Propagation

Seeds are collected in autumn, overwintered in damp sand and sown in the spring. Alders are also commonly available as hedge plants in nurseries. Older cultivated plants are best obtained from bonsai nurseries but bonsai that have already been shaped are only found on sale in exceptional cases. Wild specimens are rarely suitable for bonsai cultivation.

Pests

The alder leaf flea (*Psylla alni*) leaves behind pale dots where it has sucked, but otherwise does little damage. A bad infestation is controlled with an environmentally-friendly insecticide.

Caterpillars of the alder leaf wasp (*Croesus septentrionalis*) eat the edges of the leaves. In a bad infestation they can eat all the leaves off a large bonsai, and should therefore be removed as soon as you see them.

The alder leaf beetle (*Agelastica alni*) and its larvae are the most usual pests of the common alder and can be controlled by collecting the shiny metallic-blue adults or the black larvae. Even the conspicuous yellow eggs are easy to see and remove.

The alder fly larva (*Cryptorrynchus lapathi*) eats its way into the bark and the wood. Affected branches may die. The beetle is brownish with light diagonal stripes in its wing covers and it overwinters in the earth. The affected branches must be removed and destroyed.

Fungal diseases

Mildew can often be overlooked in the alder as its fine white covering develops on the underside of the leaves and is not very visible. The mildew fungi usually specialise in one type of plant but in alder they are supported by a non-specialist (*Phyllactinia guttata*), which can also infest other types of plant. Treat mildew with web sulphur when it first appears. It overwinters in fallen leaves so you can avoid infection by removing them.

Curling disease, caused by a fungus (*Taphrina tosquinetii*), is characterised by the formation of pale blisters and yellowy-red coloration of the affected places, which look frosted from underneath. Preventive treatment, using a fungicide containing copper, should be carried out in spring when new shoots are growing.

The eggs of the alder leaf beetle

Mating alder leaf beetles

Curling disease in the common alder (underside of the leaf)

61

Deciduous trees	# Silver birch and Downy birch

(Betula pendula/Betula pubescens)

The silver birch and the downy birch both have white trunks. Other well-known species of white-trunked trees behave in a similar way so much of what appears here can be applied to them as well. The dwarf birch is dealt with on its own in the section on shrubs.

Under normal conditions in the wild the silver birch develops into a slim, white-trunked tree with a conical crown and pendulous ends to the branches. It can reach a height of 20m (70ft) or more. When it has no leaves it is easily recognisable by the whitish warts on its branches.

The downy birch develops a rounder crown on a short white trunk without pendent branches. Its young branches have a slight covering of hairs.

Both have alternate, triangular to rhomboid leaves which often appear shortly after the blossom from mid- to late-spring, and which turn bright yellow in autumn.

Birches are monecious; pollen is wind-borne. The winged seeds ripen from early summer on and are spread by the wind.

The silver birch is found in dry, bright, mixed deciduous and coniferous woods as well as on moors, meadows and screes. The downy birch prefers damp places and is found in various mixed deciduous and coniferous woods.

As bonsai

Birch bonsai are not problem-free, as the plants do not heal very easily when cut. If cuts are not sealed carefully infections easily occur, even after some time, and can kill the affected branch. But as long as you keep a careful watch for infection, birches are otherwise relatively undemanding. A partially shaded position is preferred by both types. They are happy in a site that is sunny throughout the day if they are well watered, but they generally cannot survive in total shade. They respond to extreme heat with loss of leaves.

Both trees are sensitive to an excess of mineral salts which means that they need plenty of water; use rainwater wherever

Right: A twelve-year-old silver birch around 80cm (32in) high in autumn. Developed from a pre-shaped bonsai plant. Designer: Wolfgang Wehrend

Far right: Silver birch when the leaves are just turning, around 80cm (32in) high and twelve years old, developed from a pre-shaped bonsai plant

62

Right: Various fungal diseases in late summer and autumn cause weakened branches to die off in winter

possible. Surplus water should be allowed to drain away. The silver birch can survive short periods with no water, but will again drop its leaves.

They are tolerant of any soil, but you should renew it every two years, cutting the roots back at the same time. Silver birch loses its resistance to frost after the roots have been pruned, so it should not be repotted until the new spring growth appears.

Feed with a solid organic bonsai fertiliser every fortnight from the appearance of the first shoots until mid- to late summer.

The white outer bark needs strong growth and sun to develop well. So for the first few years your bonsai should be given a relatively large container and plenty of fertiliser. If the tree sheds its leaves normally in the autumn, it is very frost-resistant, but should be planted in the garden over the winter to be on the safe side. If the leaves do not start to change colour until the first frost, the plant should be given extra protection in temperatures below 2°C (36°F).

Shaping

A narrow crown and pendent branches are typical of the silver birch in the wild so if a natural shape is to be achieved, the Japanese styles can only serve as a rough guide. But the young branches are easily wired and the main branches do grow in a clearly upwards direction.

A birch grown as a bonsai will not produce branches that are heavy enough to give them their naturally pendulous habit but this can be achieved by wiring the new shoots downwards. The shoots which will form the crown are not pruned until early summer, as they are then long and strong enough to be styled.

Pruning

Seedlings are cut back to half their size in early summer of the second year or to about 15–20cm (6–8in) in spring of the third year. For the white outer bark to develop, the plant should be allowed to grow out in the garden for the next three years. Prune it regularly and make sure the crown does not become too dense. If it gets too thick, whole branches will die off.

With a tree that is already shaped, any branches that are not absolutely necessary for forming the crown should be removed in spring before the shoots appear. This ensures that enough sunlight reaches the trunk even when the tree is in leaf.

In younger plants, the new shoots are cut back in spring by about 20–30cm (8–12in). Older, well developed trees which already have their white bark can be cut back earlier, so that they can concentrate on producing delicate outer branches. Tips of branches that are wired down do not grow as strongly as other branches, so pruning in the silver birch must be more frequent towards the top of the tree. Birches will grow new shoots after pruning. At the end of summer these should be nipped out to prevent further growth.

Wiring

Birches should only be wired during the growing season, after the new shoots appear. Branches wired in winter will often die off in spring. Branches of one to two years, and older branches of pencil-thickness, may still be wired without damaging the bark but older branches should be anchored. Those growing in the upper third of the tree thicken particularly fast, so the wires should be changed every four weeks.

Propagation

Collect seeds in the autumn, store them in a dry place and sow them early in the year. One-year-old seedlings can be found all over the place. Two- to five-year-old saplings can also be bought in bonsai nurseries and you may come across older pre-shaped plants in nurseries.

Ready-shaped birch bonsai have recently become more widely available.

Pests

The birch beetle (*Euceraphis punctipennis*) is a greenish insect that attacks the young shoots in particular, making them wither. It is destroyed with a non-toxic aphid pesticide.

The leaf miner (*Orchestes populi*) eats holes into the leaves of birches, and its larvae cause rot which may lead to leaves dropping. They multiply fast so you need to treat them immediately. The most successful method is to collect the adults and destroy the leaves that are affected by the larvae.

Other insects living off birches, such as the gall mite (*Acaria brevitarsa*), which causes a felty covering on the underside of the leaves, the birch leaf roller (*Deporaus betulae*), which makes the leaves roll up, or the birch leaf miner (*Agromyza alnibetulae*), whose presence is characterised by holes eaten in the leaves, cause no lasting damage and are easily controlled by removing the affected leaves.

Fungal diseases

Birch rust (*Melampsoridium betulinum*) is transmitted through larches, which act as a host. It is a fungus which makes yellowy-orange spots on the underside of the leaf. These areas are yellow on the top of the leaf. Trees that are infected with birch rust drop their leaves early; in young plants this can lead to large parts of branches or even the whole tree dying off. Spray with a rust fungicide either as a preventive measure in the spring or during the attack.

Mildew is hard to identify in birches, but not uncommon. It appears in late summer as a faint grey covering on the leaves and leads to them dropping and whole branches dying off. It is most sensible to carry out preventive spraying when the shoots first appear; if mildew has already appeared, spray with a systemic fungicide.

Left: **Downy birch in spring, height around 60cm (2ft), age twelve years, developed from a pre-shaped bonsai sapling.** *Designer: Wolf D. Schudde*

65

Hornbeam

(Carpinus betulus)

The common hornbeam is closely related to the birch but its leaf shape is very similar to that of the common beech. The hornbeam is often found in hedgerows and is tolerant of pruning, which is an important requirement for bonsai. In the wild it usually develops into a smallish tree about 5–10m (15–30ft) high but it may grow bigger – up to 25m (80ft).

Hornbeams are often multiple-trunked and have an oval crown if allowed to grow naturally. With age the silver bark on the bent, twisted trunks splits lengthways creating interesting striped patterns. Male and female flowers (catkins) are produced on one plant and are wind pollinated. The seed consists of small nuts hidden in a three-lobed, winged seed case and is spread by the wind in early autumn.

The ovate leaves are serrated at the edges and are alternate. They appear relatively early, in mid- to late spring, and turn bright yellow in autumn, becoming brown and remaining on the tree often for the whole winter until the new leaves appear again.

In the wild the hornbeam occurs in various mixed woods. Very often it is also deliberately planted as a specimen tree or to make a hedge.

As bonsai

Of all native trees, the hornbeam is actually one of the favourites for bonsai. Choose a semi-shaded position: although the plant tolerates direct sunshine in the wild, the young leaves are quite sensitive to heat and not resistant to wind. In sunny sites this can lead to brown edges on the leaves in a warm and stormy spring. In a shaded position, it will only need occasional supplementary watering, so excess minerals are unlikely to build up in the soil.

The hornbeam should be watered with rainwater whenever possible, but it also tolerates tap water if it is in a position to get really wet when it does rain. In periods of low rainfall be careful to provide it with water that is low in minerals and lime, otherwise light brown edges develop on its leaves.

Take particular care with

feeding. While a pine or a juniper can survive 10 years without fertiliser, a hornbeam will start to suffer after only a year without sufficient food. Organic bonsai fertiliser in powder or pellet form is ideal. Feed every fortnight after the first new shoots appear with the amount stipulated on the packet. If, despite careful feeding, the tree shows signs of deficiencies, you can give it mineral fertiliser, but be careful as the hornbeam is sensitive to a build up of mineral salts. Stop feeding in midsummer; if you feed too much in late summer the leaves will change colour too late in the autumn and the tree will not be frost-resistant.

The hornbeam is very flexible when it comes to soil. A standard mix of loam granules (Akadama), sand and peat in proportions of 1:1:1 is ideal. Change the soil every two to three years, at the same time pruning the roots. In a healthy plant roots can be reduced by up to two thirds in the spring and in this way you quickly get a flat rootball.

Overwinter the tree in the garden, planting the rootball into the soil without the container or in a box filled with a mixture of peat and sand. Always overwinter it in a shady position. In temperatures below −10°C (14°F) the plant should be covered with foil, straw or fir branches. After mild winters make sure it is protected from late frosts.

Shaping

The hornbeam can be trained into any of the Japanese styles but the formal upright is the most commonly used. This can be achieved simply by cutting back and no wiring if you start with a plant that is not too old.

The basic shaping of a new plant can be started between the time when the buds swell and midsummer.

Pruning

The first pruning of seedlings should be carried out before the spring shoots appear in the third year.

Plants that have already been shaped can be left until three to four weeks after the shoots have appeared. Depending on what shape you are aiming for, you can wait until the shoots are 5–30cm (2–12in) long, on the basis that the longer the shoots are allowed to grow, the thicker the tree will become.

As the hornbeam produces new shoots every time it is cut back, you can achieve a delicate branch network relatively quickly. Leaf-cutting about three to four weeks after the first shoots appear is tolerated if the tree is fed well, but it will slow down thickening. From late summer the new shoots are only nipped back – the tip of the shoot is removed as soon as it has produced three to five leaves. The plant then stops growing and the last shoots have enough time to mature.

Strong branches are best removed in the spring, shortly before shoots appear, or in early summer. Wounds made in early summer heal particularly quickly.

Wiring

If you are training an older plant, whether pre-shaped or taken from the wild, you will usually have to use wire. Branches that are one or

Hornbeam

Left: **The bark of older hornbeams has an attractive pattern in the wild**

two years old can be bent easily, but because of strong thickening growth in early summer the wire must be checked regularly.

Wiring can take place any time between the first new shoots appearing in spring, and late summer.

Older branches are best trained through anchoring.

Propagation

Collect seeds in early autumn, keep them in damp sand in the fridge and sow them in the spring.

You can save a few years if you begin with an older plant.

Pre-shaped trees of various ages and roughly prepared for cultivation, are available in bonsai nurseries, often at good prices. Many bonsai nurseries also have ready trained hornbeam bonsai.

Get permission before collecting

saplings from the wild. They should be dug up during the period between the leaves changing colour in the autumn and the buds swelling in the spring.

Plants collected in autumn and winter may be protected against frost by planting the rootball deep in the garden.

Pests

Red spider mites cause yellowy speckling of the leaves, which later shrivel and drop. They should be controlled with a specific spider mite spray.

Large holes in the leaves indicate the presence of caterpillars of moths. These should be picked off by hand.

Fungal diseases

Mildew forms a floury, greyish-white covering on the top of the leaves. Spraying with a systemic fungicide in the spring just as the shoots appear is the best way to prevent it appearing. If it does appear, control it by spraying several times and remove leaves that have been badly affected.

Over the course of the year the leaves often develop brown edges. The causes are the same as those described for the beech (p.74).

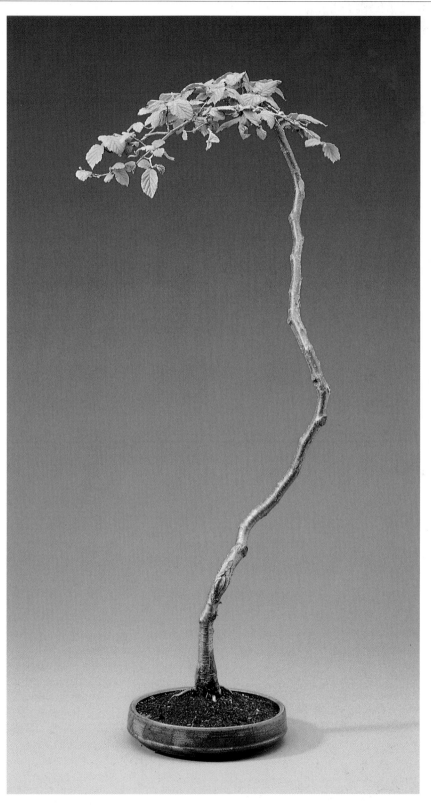

Left: **Ten-year-old hornbeam about 90cm (3ft) high, trained into the literati style from a wild seedling.** *Designer: Manfred van Eick*

Far left: **Hornbeam in spring, around 80cm (32in) high and twenty-five years old, cultivated from a nursery tree**

Sweet chestnut

(Castanea sativa)

The sweet chestnut belongs, along with the common beech and the oak, to the beech family (*Fagaceae*). Although the presence of this magnificent tree in Central Europe can be traced back to Roman times, experts are not agreed on whether the sweet chestnut was introduced to this region or occurred naturally. Because of its long history of cultivation and its regular appearance in native woods, it is dealt with here as a native tree.

The tree, which grows to 30m (100ft) high, has an irregular domed leaf canopy on a short trunk that grows rough bark with age. The broadly lanceolate, toothed, leathery, dark green leaves appear in late spring, grow to 10–20cm (4–8in) long and turn bright yellow in autumn.

The numerous male flowers are borne in long catkins and the female flowers are in small groups at the base of these catkins, which lie next to the tip of the shoots. After pollination by the wind, the edible chestnuts, surrounded by a prickly green shell, are produced.

The sweet chestnut can occur in mixed woods, but it is traditionally found on village greens, in large squares, in parks or along wide roads.

As bonsai

Because of its naturally large leaves, the sweet chestnut is seldom kept as a bonsai. However, the size of the leaves quickly reduces with increasing branching, and a well-shaped tree will develop with similar proportions to a bonsai oak, adding charm to a collection of native bonsai.

The sweet chestnut bonsai likes a sunny to semi-shady site, and its tough leaves mean that it can tolerate hot spells. As it prefers acidic soil it should be watered with rainwater and kept damp.

Choose a good permeable growing medium of loam granules (Akadama), peat and rough sand, in proportions of 2:1:1 by weight. Feed well from mid-spring to early summer with a solid organic bonsai fertiliser and from mid- to late summer with a mineral fertiliser that is rich in potassium.

Depending on how developed your bonsai is, new branch growth can be encouraged by pruning two to four weeks after the first spring shoots appear and, in cultivated plants, the leaves can be trimmed after another two weeks.

The sweet chestnut is damaged by hard frosts. It should therefore either be overwintered in a frost-free place, such as by a window in the garage, or planted in the garden without its container and covered with leaves or straw at the onset of cold weather. The protection can be removed again when the frosts are over. Overwintering on a balcony, depending on its construction and exposure to the weather, can be risky.

Shaping

The sweet chestnut's natural habit makes the broom style particularly easy. The formal upright style and the various multiple trunk styles are also possibilities. The final size should be 60cm (2ft) or more because of its relatively large leaves.

Pruning

Young plants are cut back for the first time in the third year, when the plant has reached at least two thirds of the planned height.

The first pruning determines the

height of the trunk, so at this point the plant is reduced to a third of the planned final height. Shoots that appear after this should be cut back, either hard or moderately, depending on their position in the planned branch system.

If you have to remove a strong branch, this is best done in late spring when the leaves appear. Fresh cuts seal most quickly at this time of year.

Wiring

Wiring is carried out in the spring after the first pruning, and also during the summer.

Only branches up to two years old can be wired without the risk of permanent scars, so older branches should be anchored.

Propagation

Collect seeds in mid-autumn, keep them in damp sand in the fridge and sow them in the spring.

Bonsai nurseries seldom sell young plants, pre-shaped plants or cultivated bonsai.

Pests and insects

Red spider mites make yellowy-green spots on the leaves, and white dots found on the leaf undersides are their shed skins. They should be controlled with a spider mite spray.

Leaf mites usually only occur singly and can be washed off with a strong jet of water.

Walnut

(Juglans regia)

The walnut has a short trunk, which only develops bark with age, has a sparse, large, round leaf-covering and reaches a height of 10–20m (30–70ft). The alternate, large, feathered leaves appear in late spring with the flowers. In autumn there is often no real change in colour, just a slight yellowing.

The male blossom is formed in clumps in strong catkins but the female flowers, which appear separately, are very simple and green. The tree is pollinated by the wind, and the fruit, walnuts, are surrounded by a green shell and ripen in early autumn.

Right: Walnut in
spring

As bonsai

The walnut is very rarely trained as a bonsai because of its huge leaves but it is included here because of its long history as a cultivated plant.

Walnuts are happy in either sunny sites or partial shade but should be protected from strong wind and late frost, which can damage the first shoots. It can be watered all year round with hard tap water.

The best potting compost for this tree is a mixture, not too fine, of loam granules, sand and peat in proportions of 2:1:1. The best time for repotting is in mid-spring but, when changing the soil, do not remove more than a third of the roots. Feed well with solid organic bonsai fertiliser from mid-spring to midsummer.

The walnut is not particularly frost resistant and should therefore spend the winter planted in the garden without its container. It should be covered in temperatures below –5°C (23°F). Balconies are unlikely to be in a suitable situation for overwintering walnuts.

Shaping

The walnut is very difficult to shape because of its large, feathery leaves. The style that it should follow is sometimes only clear in winter when it has dropped its leaves.

Its somewhat chaotic leaf covering can be given some order by cutting the leaves in half or even removing them completely.

Good proportions between leaf and trunk size are only attained once the tree reaches a certain height.

Pruning

The walnut puts forth shoots relatively late in the year. Depending on their stage of development, trees which have just been shaped produce branches 10–20cm (4–8in) long – young plants with few branches, in relatively large containers – or very small branches about 5–10cm (2–4in) long. In both cases the shoots are very strong and almost as thick as a pencil.

In a container the walnut will usually stop growing after it has put forth once, unless pruning or leaf-cutting is carried out. The spring shoots should therefore be trimmed back, at the latest three weeks after the first leaves appear, to one to three leaves. In order to encourage side shoots, even branches that don't appear to be growing in length should have the strong bud at the end removed, at the very least. The feathering on

the leaves can also be reduced to two to four feathers. Feed well and new shoots will appear after about four weeks.

Wiring

In walnuts even the young branches are thick and will show resistance if their position is altered. Strong wire should therefore be used even if the branches are only a year old.

After the plant is put into a bonsai container its thickening slows considerably, so there is less danger of in-growing, but any damage that does occur is visible for a long time. Anchoring wires are therefore preferred.

Propagation

Collect seeds in autumn, keep them over the winter in damp sand in the fridge and sow them in the spring. Wild seedlings suitable for cultivation are very rare. Saplings are seldom sold and pre-shaped or cultivated plants hardly ever. Your best bet is to search around to find your own seeds.

Pests

Red spider mites cause a grey-green colouring of the leaves and possibly leaf fall. Control them with a spider mite spray.

Fungal diseases

Blackish-brown marks on the leaves are a sign of leaf spot disease, which should be treated with an appropriate spray.

Left: **Walnut in winter, height around 40cm (16in), eight years old, cultivated from a pre-shaped bonsai**

Common beech

(Fagus sylvatica)

This very tenacious tree is one of the most important components of many European deciduous forests.

Through its ability to survive on low levels of light, the beech is able to develop and grow strong even in thick woods, eventually overshadowing everything itself. It allows very little light through, so that few other plants are able to develop under it, the only ones being those that have already produced leaves when the beech becomes covered in its thick foliage in late spring.

The common beech has green foliage but its red relation, the copper beech (*Fagus sylvatica* var. *purpurea*), can also be found in the wild.

In parks and gardens you will find it with different habits and varying leaf shapes.

This tree, which grows up to 30m (100ft) high in woodland, has a long trunk with a leaf canopy that covers only the top third of its total height. A solitary tree develops a domed leaf canopy, with some branches reaching almost to the ground.

The silvery grey bark remains smooth even in old trees.

The tree is monoecious, flowers inconspicuously and is pollinated by the wind, enclosing its edible seeds (beech nuts) in a hard triangular shell until autumn.

The alternate, pointed oval leaves appear often only towards the end of spring, from conspicuous, long, pointed cinnamon-coloured buds. They have velvety lashes, are dark green on top and smooth, later becoming almost bald. In autumn its colour changes from orangey-yellow to yellow and then turns brown with the leaves often staying on the tree all winter and only being shed shortly before the new shoots appear.

As with most trees, the beech lives in symbiosis with fungi.

As bonsai

As a bonsai the beech prefers a partly shaded position which is protected from the midday sun and from too much wind. It is sensitive to lime so should be given rainwater or water low in minerals. If you can only use tap water, the tree should be watered so much that most of the water runs off again, taking with it excess minerals. The more water the tree needs, the greater the danger of excess lime in the soil, so take care that not too much water is lost through evaporation by providing protection in windy or hot weather.

From the time the new shoots appear you should feed your beech well with a fertiliser containing a relatively high proportion of potassium. This enables the tree to build up a better protection against evaporation. Brown edges often appear on the leaves in summer and are a sign of lack of potassium, or are caused by too high a concentration of lime in the soil.

A mixture of Japanese loam granules, sand and peat, in proportions of 1:1:1 makes a good soil.

The beech should be repotted at least every two years in spring, and the roots should be pruned at the same time.

Overwinter the tree in a shady spot in the garden, removing its container and burying the rootball in the earth, or on a balcony in a box filled with peat and sand.

During long periods of frost and temperatures below −10°C (14°F), the tree should be covered with twigs, straw or plastic sheet.

Cultivation

Of the Japanese styles, the formal upright corresponds most closely with the natural shape of the beech, but most of the other styles are possible as well. Wild saplings or prepared plants can be given their first basic shaping between the time the buds begin to swell and towards the end of summer.

Pruning

Seedlings are cut back before the new shoots appear in spring of their third year. Trees that are already shaped and have just been repotted are cut back as soon as the first shoots have fully developed. If you do not want longer branches, you may leave only one or two leaves on the tree.

Older trees with established roots can be cut back before the new shoots have developed fully, leaving only one or two leaves in this case as well.

Within about three weeks the beech will produce new shoots, which can also be cut back to one or two leaves. The leaves remaining on the tree grow very large from now on so, if the tree is healthy and well fed, you can

proceed with leaf-cutting after a further two weeks. But be careful because direct sunlight will harm the tree when it has no leaves, so put it in a shady spot until the next shoots appear.

The top branches are usually more productive than the lower ones so pruning is carried out a bit earlier at the top of the tree than it is in the lower part. The winter buds in the upper third are also usually stronger and the branching is better developed than further down. This can be compensated for by greatly reducing the upper third of the crown in the winter, or the spring before the new growth appears. Strong branches should be cut back in the spring shortly before the shoots appear, and the cuts sealed with a wound sealant.

Wiring

Wiring a beech requires a great deal of care, as the bark is damaged easily and any wires that become too tight will leave permanent scars. In early summer there is a sudden thickening growth and wires that are not checked every few days can quickly grow in. If possible, only the branches that are a year old

should be wired; other branches should be trained by anchoring.

Propagation

Collect seeds in autumn, put them in damp sand and keep them in the fridge until spring, when you can sow them. Cut the plant back after two years at the earliest.

You may find very good starter plants on walks in the woods but you must get permission to remove them. Wild seedlings have a greater chance of survival if they can spend a couple of years in the garden after being gathered. Regular rough pruning can be carried out during this time.

Bonsai nurseries should have a good selection of beeches both ready-shaped plants, which have already spent several years in a container, and others that are not in containers but are ready to be cultivated.

Pests

A woolly, white substance on the underside of the leaf is a sign of the beech aphid (*Phyllaphis fagi*). It overwinters as eggs on the buds and branches, appears in spring, often in great numbers, and causes the leaves to roll up. Its sticky excretions may encourage soot fungus. Treat this with a systemic insecticide; it may be prevented by using tar oil in winter.

Other insects living on the beech cause little or no damage to the plant, so you can either ignore them, in the case of the gall mite and the beech gall mosquito, or remove them by hand, as in the case of the beech spring mite (*Rhynchaenus fagi*) and the caterpillar of the beech frost moth (*Operophthera fagata*).

Above: **In bonsai containers, as in the wild, most trees live symbiotically with fungi**

Below: **Beech fruit and leaves**

Premature browning which often appears on parts of the leaves may be caused by the following:

Mineral salt damage: the edges of the leaves turn evenly brown. This often occurs after warm, dry days, during which the plant has been watered mainly with tap water. This phenomenon can be avoided by using rainwater.

Lack of nutrients: The veins of the leaves are dark green, the leaf blade is yellowy-green, the edges of the leaves often have irregular, wide brown patches. Acute lack of nutrients can often be rectified by feeding with a good mineral fertiliser. (See also p.20–23.)

A lack of nutrients and a deterioration in the quality of the soil can be caused by watering the tree wrongly. If the above symptoms occur despite feeding, the soil should be changed.

Fungal diseases

Leaf-browning, where the tips of the leaves turn brown, is caused by the fungus *Apiognomonia errabunda*, and only rarely kills the plant. The fungus is spread through spraying with water.

It should be treated with a fungicide containing copper, such as Bordeaux mixture.

Above: European beech in the windswept form, around 50cm (20in) high and fifteen years old, cultivated from a wild seedling. *Designer: Gerhard Paschke*

Below: European beech in the cascade style, around 40cm (16in) high and ten years old, cultivated from a wild seedling

Common ash

(Fraxinus excelsior)

The common ash is the only indigenous example of the genus *Fraxinus*, but the Manna ash (*Fraxinus ornus*) is also widely grown and you will find other species in parks and gardens as well. In the wild this magnificent tree reaches a height of up to 40m (130ft) and develops a huge round crown on a short trunk.

The purplish flowers develop in clusters, open before the leaves do and occur in both monoecious and dioecious forms. They are pollinated by the wind and develop into bunches of winged nuts, which ripen in the autumn, and fall very late, sometimes in the following spring.

The alternate, unpaired, feathered leaves develop in late spring from a strong black bud and drop in the autumn after the first frost without changing colour.

The light grey bark is smooth at first but later acquires shallow vertical cracks.

Right: The fruit of the ash hang in thick bunches

Far right: Ash in late summer, around 70cm (28in) high and twelve years old, cultivated from a pre-shaped bonsai

As bonsai

The ash bonsai thrives in a light, sunny position, but can also be kept in partial shade and, if it is watered sufficiently, it will easily tolerate a site that is exposed to wind. The soil can consist of a mix of loam granules, sand and peat in proportions of 3:1:1 in weight, but other mixes are also possible.

Young, undeveloped plants should be repotted at least every two years. Those that already have well-developed branches can tolerate less frequent changes of soil. The roots can be pruned at the same time as repotting; if repotting is carried out in spring, up to three quarters of the roots can be removed, so that you quickly achieve a flat rootball.

The plant should be kept consistently well watered: you can give it tap water. On hot and windy days the ash uses large quantities of liquid, so you will have to water it several times a day.

Feed it with solid organic bonsai fertiliser, such as rape pellets, from the start of the shoots appearing until the beginning of late summer. Liquid mineral fertiliser is also acceptable in exact quantities, and is preferable to organic fertiliser in cool weather.

Overwinter the tree in the garden in a shady spot, with the rootball planted in the soil without a container, or on a balcony in a box filled with a mix of peat and sand.

After the shoots appear in spring, the ash is very sensitive to cold and should therefore be protected from late frosts.

Cultivation

Of the Japanese styles the broom is nearest to the ash's natural shape, but the upright style is also suitable.

New branches are not readily put forth by the ash and they always remain relatively thick, so it will never achieve the fine branching found in an elm.

Because of its relatively large, feathered leaves, the branches should be appropriately spaced and you should aim for an eventual height of over 50cm (20in).

If possible, young trees should be shaped when they are in leaf, from late spring to midsummer, because large cuts heal best during this time and side shoots will also often produce new branches within the same year.

Pruning

In their third year, saplings are cut back for the first time before the shoots appear in spring to one third of the planned total height of the bonsai. Of the two shoots that develop, one will become the continuation of the trunk, while the other will form the first side branch through early pruning. The shoot that forms the continuation of the trunk can be cut back again if it grows strongly in the same year.

In trees that have already been shaped, at least the first bud,

which is always quite well formed, should be removed from all branches which are to produce further shoots but do not need to grow any thicker. You should do this before the new spring shoots appear otherwise only these strong buds will develop, preventing the tree from branching out further.

Leaf-cutting helps branch division and can be carried out along with the first pruning in healthy trees.

When your tree has almost reached the desired final height, nip back the new shoots in the upper third of the leaf covering as soon as one or two pairs of leaves have formed. In the lower area, leave the shoots until they reach a length of four to six pairs of leaves and then cut them back to one or two pairs. Later shoots can then be cut back after the third pair of leaves has developed.

Wiring

The wood of the ash is very hard, so only one-year-old branches can be wired without damaging the bark. Older branches can be trained in the desired direction by using anchoring wires.

Propagation

Collect seeds from late summer onwards, keep them in damp sand in the fridge and sow them in the spring. The first pruning should be carried out in the third year.

Older plants that are suitable for bonsai are seldom found in the wild. Young plants and prepared specimens are sometimes available in specialist bonsai nurseries and in rare cases you will find pre-shaped trees on offer.

Pests

The following occur from time to time:

The slimy larvae of the ash caterpillar (*Cionus fraxini*) eat holes into the underside of the leaf. Remove the affected leaves.

The ash leaf fly (*Psylopsis fraxini*) first causes a yellowy patch where it sucks the leaves which later turn dark brown and curl up. The affected leaves should be removed or, in a bad case, sprayed with a suitable insecticide.

The caterpillar of the ash fork moth (*Prays curtisellus*) starts by eating through from the top of the leaves, which it then then spins together. The second generation of caterpillars goes for the buds and the tips of the shoots. It forces its way into these in the autumn and overwinters inside, eating its way out in spring. You can prevent the moth from spreading by removing the affected part of the plant.

The ash beetle (*Hylesinus fraxini*), around 3mm (¹/₈in) long and brightly coloured, eats the bark away leaving crusty galls. Treatment is with a suitable spray.

The tree may also be affected by the caterpillar of the willow moth (*Cossus cossus*), which eats into the trunk in the summer and overwinters for several years in the holes it has made. The caterpillar grows up to 10cm (4in) long and as thick as a finger, and can completely hollow out a strong ash bonsai from the inside. If you discover the hole through which it has entered early enough – a floury substance will appear around it – the caterpillar can be removed with a piece of wire.

Far left: The ash in autumn with its leaves turning faintly yellow. This specimen is around 60cm (2ft) high and twelve years old and was cultivated from a pre-shaped bonsai

Left: This gall is a sign of the ash beetle

Left: Frost damage on the spring shoots of the ash

Common crab apple

(Malus sylvestris)

The crab apple is a small tree with a short trunk and, with age, produces a wide oval, often irregular, leaf covering, which is flat on top.

The smooth trunk can develop a crumbling bark in older plants.

The flowers, which are reddish as buds and later white, develop on short shoots after the first leaves appear in late spring. The flowering stems and sepals are usually bald, but not in cultivated plants. After insect pollination, small, rather bitter apples up to 4cm (1½in) across develop, often in great numbers.

The elliptic leaves, serrated at the edges, are slightly felty on the underside. In autumn they turn from dirty yellowy-brown to light orange.

Unlike cultivated apple trees, the crab apple develops short prickly shoots but is otherwise difficult to distinguish from some cultivated types and their hybrids. It is therefore described here along with apple trees in general.

As bonsai

The apple tree bonsai likes a sunny, airy position and a lot of water. In hot weather it is the first of all tree species to droop due to lack of water. But the apple does like lime, so it can be given hard tap water.

A standard bonsai soil of loam granules, sand and peat in proportions of 1:1:1 serves as good growing medium. The container should be large enough for water to be stored in the soil in sufficient quantities to cater for the apple's high water requirement.

A solid organic fertiliser, such as pellets, should be given from late spring until towards the end of summer.

The flowers should be protected from late frosts. Fruits develop in great quantities if two apple trees that blossom at the same time are kept together, as apples will usually only produce fruit if they

Right: **Apple tree in its natural shape in winter, around 40cm (16in) high and ten years old, cultivated from a seedling**

Left: Fruit only
grows in abundance
on the apple tree if
it is cross-pollinated
with another tree. To
ensure this happens,
two trees have been
planted here in the
same container

are cross-pollinated. The more fruits that develop, the less the tree grows, but if the tree bears a moderate crop of fruit, and it is pruned regularly throughout the growing season, it will continue to put forth new shoots until late summer.

The apple tree is overwintered in the garden, with the rootball in the earth without its container, or on a balcony in a box filled with peat and sand.

Right: **The fruit can be very attractive**

Cultivation

Apple trees imported from Japan have a very lumpy appearance: a short, thick trunk and boughs that branch out very little but are covered in flowers or fruit. These small trees bear little resemblance to our natural apple tree.

Apple trees, like many other trees, can be grown in the ordinary broom style or the upright style. The best time to shape a new plant is between the swelling of the buds in the spring and midsummer.

Pruning

Depending on the age of the tree, pruning can be carried out when the shoots are 5–10cm (2–4in) long. At least one leaf should be left on to discourage the flowering shoots from growing too long. After heavy pruning in the summer the tree will still sometimes produce flowers that should really appear next year, so fruit that is almost ripe and fresh blossoms appear on the same tree together.

Older branches are cut back in the spring at the same time as the new shoots as wounds heal better then.

Wiring

Apple trees are easily wired but only one-year-old branches can be bent in the desired direction without difficulty. Stronger branches are, therefore, best trained with anchoring wires.

Propagation

Collect seeds in autumn, remove the flesh of the fruit and keep them over the winter in damp sand in the fridge. Sow them in the spring.

Crab apples are very rarely found in nurseries so cultivated trees will usually have been grown from seed. But there are many types of apple available in specialist bonsai nurseries, with differing leaf and fruit colours and different sizes of fruit.

Pests

The fruit tree mite (*Panonychus ulmi*) first causes the leaves to turn yellowy in patches and then greeny-brown, and later to drop in

a bad case. In mid- to late summer it is at its most prolific, and it is often first noticed then. Treatment with natural predators seldom produces effective results, but a special spray, available in garden centres, can be applied before new spring growth appears and will control the mite until the summer. But a poisonous systemic insecticide is the only long-lasting treatment. Ask which sort to use in a garden centre.

The yellowy-green larvae of the apple leaf aphid (*Psylla mali*) suck the sap from the young green parts of the tree causing crinkly leaves which then fall off. A mild attack can be treated with a strong jet of water but in bad cases a suitable contact insecticide spray can also be used.

The green apple leaf aphid (*Aphis pomi*), often found in great numbers, drains the sap from young shoots which shrivel and later die. The tree must be pruned heavily and then washed down with a strong jet of water but you can also use a non-toxic spray in addition to this.

The woolly aphid (*Eriosoma lanigerum*) sucks on woody parts of the tree causing furry growths to form and is easily recognised by its furry white secretions, under which it hides. It overwinters in the root area and goes on sucking there in mild winters, causing the roots to become thick and bulging. An aphid insecticide can control it but it is often necessary to spray well several times, also in the root area. If woolly aphids have already appeared once, the bonsai should be treated regularly, even in the following year.

Weevils, often a pretty metallic green, eat holes into the leaves and usually the buds as well. The larvae live in the soil feeding off the roots. An attack can, in most cases, be controlled by picking off the weevils and occasionally checking the roots. In a bad case you can also use an insecticide, which can be bought in a garden centre.

The larvae of the little apple leaf mining moth (*Lyonetia clerkella*) eat into the leaf leaving a yellowish, easily recognisable meandering trail. Collect and destroy the affected leaves.

The caterpillars of the apple tree web moth are recognisable by their web, within which any number of them sit, eating the tree. In a short period of time they can eat a bonsai completely bald. Controlling them is easy: simply remove the caterpillars and their web.

Fungal diseases

Apple scab on the leaves causes olive green patches, which later turn brown, spread and lead to the leaves dropping. The fungus overwinters in the dropped leaves and can be controlled by removing the old leaves and spraying the new shoots several times with an apple scab treatment (ask in a garden centre).

Fruit tree canker can be recognised in its initial stages by black spots on the bark, which often spread slowly but consistently, with the affected places later swelling up into a canker. The infection usually gets into the tree through wounds and can be controlled early on by removing the affected parts of the tree. In the autumn the tree should then be sprayed with a copper fungicide.

Apple mildew is easily recognised by a white coating on young shoots and leaves. You can prevent attack by spraying the new shoots carefully with a mildew treatment. Once it has occurred though, the fungus can only be stopped from developing further by spraying. In a mild case you can prevent it from spreading by removing the affected leaves.

Bacterial diseases

Fireblight is characterised by the leaves of young shoots suddenly wilting and turning brown. These remain on the branches, becoming blackish-brown, and the whole tree eventually dies. In certain areas fireblight is a notifiable disease and must be reported. This bacterial disease can only be controlled by destroying the whole tree.

Viral diseases

Viral diseases are also controlled only by destroying the whole tree.

Apple mosaic virus causes yellow spots and lines on the leaves, which later turn brown and drop off.

Rubbery wood disease is apparent when the branches droop down and the wood is soft and gives when you squeeze it.

Flat Limb causes shoots that are several years old to develop a smooth or furrowed bark.

Viral diseases are extremely rare in bonsai, as they are almost always transmitted by grafting, and show immediately in young plants. Although apple trees can get a lot of illnesses, they are no more susceptible than other trees if cared for properly.

Left: **This apple tree in the Japanese style stands out because of its particularly thick trunk**

85

Wild pear

(Pyrus pyraster)

Like the apple, the pear has also been one of the most important cultivated plants in Europe since time immemorial. Many hybrids have been formed between the wild pear tree and the cultivated version, making it almost impossible to distinguish between the two, so they are dealt with here as one species.

The slowly growing pear tree gradually develops an upright oval, often also irregular crown on a strong trunk, which can reach a height of up to 20m (70ft) and whose bark forms a pattern of rectangles.

The flowers, which appear with or occasionally before the new shoots, are white, and are pollinated by insects. The pears are usually small and green, sometimes reddish. Like the apple, the pear needs to be cross-pollinated to produce fruit.

The ends of the shoots are pointed like thorns. The leaves, which are oval and alternate, are dark green on top and light green underneath, and the edges are finely serrated. In the autumn they turn from bright orange to dark red.

As bonsai

The pear likes a sunny or partially shaded, airy position. It does not need as much water as the apple, but it also likes lime and can therefore be watered with hard tap water. It should be fertilised well with a solid organic bonsai fertiliser from the end of spring until the last few weeks of summer.

A loose coarse-grained mix of loam granules, peat and sand in proportions of 1:1:1 by weight is a good growing medium. Young plants, whose trunks and branches have yet to develop, should have their soil changed every two years; older cultivated plants need it to be changed only every three to five years. The roots should be pruned at the same time.

Overwinter the tree in a light but shady position in the garden with the rootball planted in the soil without its container, or on a balcony in a box filled with a mixture of peat and sand.

Cultivation

The wild pear is rarely kept as a bonsai so the few examples to be found add something quite special to a bonsai collection. It is possible to grow it in any style desired and it develops increasingly smaller leaves as the branches subdivide.

Pruning

The pear tree grows very slowly, so in order to keep it producing new growth over the year it must be pruned several times during the growing season.

Young plants should be pruned later, when the shoots have ten leaves on, and older plants earlier, when the shoots have about five leaves.

The last pruning should be carried out in the last few weeks of late summer and any new shoots that follow this should be nipped back.

Stronger branches are removed during the peak growth period from late spring to midsummer; during this time large cuts seal more quickly.

Wiring

Branches over three years old should not be wired, but should be trained by anchoring.

Thickening is quite slow, so as long as wires are not attached too tightly in the spring they can remain on the tree for the entire growing season.

Propagation

Collect the fruit in the autumn, remove the flesh and keep the seeds in damp sand in the fridge over the winter. Sow them in the spring.

Young plants are very seldom

Right: **Leaf of the pear tree, top and underside**

Far right: **Pear, presented at an exhibition**

found in nurseries, neither are prepared or cultivated ones; if you find one do not hesitate to buy it. Wild seedlings suitable for bonsai are found in few areas, and are rare even then.

Pests

The pear pox mite *(Phytoptus pyri)* makes red pock marks on the leaves, these later turn brown then black. Control it by collecting the affected leaves.

The larvae of the pear leaf flea *(Psylla pirisuga)* and the pear sucker *(Psylla piri Mats)*. suck on rolled up young leaves. Spray with an aphid spray such as Malathion.

The larvae of the floury pear aphid *(Sappaphis piri)* make the leaves roll up lengthways. They sit on the underside of the leaf surrounded by a powdery secretion. The affected leaves can be collected and destroyed, but in a bad case they will need to be sprayed with an aphid spray.

Fungal and bacterial diseases

Pear scab causes olive green, later dark brown, patches on the leaves, which eventually drop. The tree can be treated in spring with a spray.

Pear rust, quite a rare disease, causes orangey-red patches on the top of the leaves. At the same place on the underside orange pustules appear with brownish tumours that are stringy when they burst open. Like other rust infections, pear rust requires an intermediate host. Control with a spray for rust fungus.

Fireblight (see Crab apple p.85).

Common oak and Durmast oak

(Quercus robur/Quercus petraea)

Right: Oaks also live in symbiosis with fungi

The oak was greatly admired by many nations in the past. The Greeks dedicated it to Zeus, the Germanic nations dedicated it to Donar and the Romans to Jupiter. It was said to be capable of many things – people believed that you could hear the voices of the gods in the rustling leaves, that you could foretell the future in the crevices and grooves of the bark, and that goblins lived under its roots. Its role in European mythology is only matched by the lime tree.

If it is allowed to grow freely, the common oak has a short but thick, barked trunk, which carries a broadly spreading crown. The branches are very bent, gnarled, irregular and relatively sparse.

Separate male and female flowers are borne on the same tree and appear with the leaves. The male flowers are inconspicuous greeny-yellow catkins and hang near the bushy female flowers, which cluster together; pollination is by the wind. On the common oak the fruit (acorns) are positioned in groups of three on a long stem

Right: Leaf of durmast oak (above), fruit and leaf of common oak (below)

Far right: Oak in autumn, around 50cm (20in) high and fifteen years old. *Designer: Hermann Pieper*

and on the durmast oak they are in clusters directly attached to the branch, with no stem. They ripen from early to mid-autumn.

The irregularly lobed, alternate leaves appear later than any other tree. On the common oak they are are short-stemmed and have two lobes forming a heart shape at the base of the leaf. On the durmast oak they are long-stemmed.

In the wild both species occur in mixed oak woods but are also not uncommon in coppices and hedgerows. The common oak is also at home in meadows and evergreen mixed forests.

As bonsai

Oaks have no particular requirements with regard to position, but should not be kept in too shady a spot. A couple of hours of sun will encourage their good health. They can thrive in quite extreme conditions, such as in direct sunlight or on a very windy balcony. The common oak has a relatively high tolerance of mineral salts and likes a slightly limy soil so it can be watered with hard tap water.

Feed it well from mid-spring to late summer with a solid organic fertiliser, such as rape pellets. Liquid mineral fertiliser also gives good results.

Young plants need new soil every two years in order to develop as quickly as possible. The soil can consist of different elements: common oak likes sandy soil as much as it likes loamy soil. For example, you can use a mix of *Akadama* (Japanese loam granules), sand and peat in proportions of 1:1:1.

The best time to repot is

Below: Oak in autumn, around 90cm (3ft) high and thirty years old, cultivated from a wild sapling

between late winter and mid-spring. Oaks should never be repotted in the autumn: if they lose too many of their storage roots when their roots are pruned, they will starve until the spring.

A hard winter reveals how sensitive bonsai oaks are to frost. The rootball should always be well protected and weakened trees, those that have had several leaf-cuttings for example, are best overwintered in a frost-free position. In any case, all the leaves should be removed to avoid the danger of fungal infection, and the tree should be sprayed with a fungicide containing copper. Healthy trees that have developed normally are overwintered outside with the rootball planted in the garden soil in a shady position, or on a balcony in a box filled with peat and sand. When the growing season begins again in the spring, the oak should be protected from late frosts.

Cultivation

The oak can be shaped in any of the Japanese styles but none of these closely resembles its natural habit. So if a typical oak shape is desired, the Japanese styles will give only limited assistance in training.

The basic shaping of a new plant is best undertaken between the end of spring and midsummer.

Pruning

Seedlings are cut back for the first time in the spring of the third year. The common oak reacts very well to pruning. The upper shoots impede the lower ones when they grow so branching in the upper third of the tree should be reduced in spring to no more than the degree of branching lower down. In most cases, only the buds at the end of each shoot will actually develop but if you remove these in spring, before the new shoots appear, the side buds will also develop, so that the branching is improved.

Plants that have just been shaped but whose trunks have not yet developed to their best should be allowed to grow until the first new shoots in spring are at least 20–30cm (8–12in) long. However, the first pruning should take place not later than three weeks after the shoots appear. The common oak will grow new shoots again within three weeks of each pruning, but only if it is properly fed. If growth does come to a standstill, it can be encouraged again by cutting the

Left: Larvae of the oak leaf wasp

Centre: The oak dwarf aphid sucks on the underside of the leaf and produces obvious yellow patches on the top of the leaf

Right: Shield lice can completely cover young branches

leaves. A well fertilised older oak can cope with two leaf-cuttings a year. At each leaf-cutting you need to be careful that the growth in the top third of the tree is not too dominant. To prevent this it is a good idea to cut back the upper branches earlier, or harder than the lower ones.

Wiring

Young branches are easily wired and older branches can be trained well with anchoring wires. The best time to wire is when the shoots start to appear in spring. Branches appearing throughout the year can be wired during the same growing season, as soon as they harden.

Propagation

Seeds which have been collected in autumn are overwintered in damp sand in the fridge and sown in early spring. The first pruning can be carried out in the third year.

Unshaped common oaks of different ages are available from specialist bonsai nurseries. They

make the best raw material for developing into a bonsai oak. You should only take plants from the wild in exceptional cases; if you have permission to do so, you should dig it up in the spring, about four weeks before the shoots appear.

Pests

Various wasps cause tumours or blisters on the leaves of the oak. An attack causes no damage to the tree's health but does make it rather unattractive to look at. Removing the affected leaves is sufficient control.

The greeny-black, transparent, slug-like larvae of the oak leaf wasp eat holes into the leaves, which should then be removed to control the infestation.

The yellowy-green oak dwarf aphid (*Phylloxera coccinea*) makes yellow patches on the top and underside of the leaves, which eventually drop. The aphids live on the underside of the leaf and can be controlled with a systemic insecticide or contact pesticides, such as malathion.

Other aphids rarely appear in significant numbers, so treatment is not necessary.

The caterpillars of the oak procession spider (*Thaumetopoea processionea*) eat away parts of the tree causing substantial damage, but they are easy to spot and can easily be gathered. Be careful, as their hairs tend to fall out and can cause inflammation of the skin and mucous membranes.

Fungal diseases

Powdery mildew (*Microsphaera alphitoides*) usually produces its white covering on young leaves but is also common on older leaves. The affected leaves may be misshapen and there is no further growth. The fungus overwinters in the buds and infests the new shoots in the spring. This is probably the most common disease of the oak and is controlled at the onset of white patches by spraying several times with systemic sulphur or other powdery mildew preparations. Preventive spraying can be carried out in spring when the shoots appear.

Rowan or Mountain ash

(Sorbus aucuparia)

Far right: **Rowan in autumn, around 60cm (2ft) high and twelve years old, cultivated from a pre-shaped bonsai**

Below: **Rowan in spring**

This tree, which rarely grows over 12m (40ft) high, usually has a domed, fairly sparse, leaf covering. At the end of spring or beginning of summer the alternate, unpaired, feathered leaves appear from large, hairy, blackish-brown buds. Autumn colour varies from yellow to red.

The white flowers which stand in domed sprays develop shortly after the leaves and are pollinated by insects to form berries which are red when ripe, 7–9mm ($\frac{1}{4}$–$\frac{3}{8}$in) in size and are much loved by birds.

The trunk remains smooth for a long time, but the flat bark can split open with age.

The rowan is found in many mixed woods. It is also not uncommon on high moorland and heaths, and in mountainous areas up to heights of 2000m (6,500ft). It is often planted on streets and in hedgerows.

As bonsai

The rowan bonsai prefers a semi-shaded to sunny position. The fruit develop on the tip of the shoots in the upper branches from the eighth year.

Ideally the tree should be kept damp; it is sensitive to lime so it is best to use rainwater or other water that is low in minerals. Lack of water is apparent early on by wilting in the new shoots. In heat or strong wind the rowan's need for water is huge, but if it is given enough water it can withstand both conditions.

The rowan has no particular preference for soil but it should be given new soil at least every two years in the spring, pruning the roots at the same time.

Feed your tree with organic powder fertiliser or with rape pellets, from when the shoots start to appear until the end of summer. Prepare it for the autumn with a low-nitrate fertiliser high in potassium, between the end of summer and the beginning of autumn.

Rowans grow naturally in mountain areas and so are

naturally very frost-resistant. As a bonsai, however, they should be overwintered planted out in the garden, or in a box on a balcony filled with peat and sand.

Cultivation

The rowan is not easy to shape: its long feathery leaves make it look more like a palm than a native tree and it is very difficult to encourage branching out. The tree should be allowed to grow to at least 50–60cm (20–24in) high to counteract these problems.

The basic shaping of a new plant is carried out during the time between the buds swelling in the spring and midsummer.

Pruning

The earliest seedlings are cut back is when they are two years old. They are then left to grow in the open and replanted every two to three years. Only when the trunk has reached a reasonable thickness should it be planted in a container and cultivated.

To encourage the development of side shoots, remove all the buds at the tips in spring before the shoots appear, and cut back the branches so that the crown does not become too heavy. When pruning, remember that the leaves are very long and feathered.

New side branches only develop with the first shoots in spring. They grow relatively slowly in relation to the lead shoots so they should not

be cut back over the course of the year. The shoots at the end of the main branches are cut back by at least two thirds when the shoots are between 10 and 20cm (4–8in), depending on their position in the tree. Each time a shoot is pruned only one bud grows, usually the one nearest to the wound.

The last pruning should be carried out four weeks before the end of summer. Branches putting forth later are nipped back – the tips of the shoots are removed as soon as two or three leaves have developed.

Wiring

As the rowan's new shoots grow very strongly upwards, it is very difficult not to have to resort to wiring in cultivation. Branches up to two years old are still easy to wire but anchoring wires are preferable on the rowan.

Propagation

The seeds germinate best if they have passed through a bird's gut. You might find seedlings in your own garden, usually near a fence where birds have been, and can use these as your starting plants.

Plants that are already several years old can be found in bonsai nurseries.

Fungal diseases

Rowan rust, is a fungus that is common where rowan and the alternate host, juniper, grow together. It is characterised first by yellowy patches on the top of the leaves; these later turn reddish to brown. In the same place on the underside of the leaves whitish grey pustules appear which spread yellow spores. Treat with Bordeaux mixture.

Powdery mildew is visible on the rowan as a whitish covering on the top of the leaves and can be controlled with systemic sulphur, as in other types of tree.

Brown edges on the leaves are a sign of lime levels in the soil being too high. You can avoid this by using water low in mineral salts, such as rainwater.

Small-leaved lime

(Tilia cordata)

The lime is a stately tree often found lining streets in towns and cities and along long avenues. Its name actually has nothing to do with the citrus fruit but comes from the Old English word 'lind', lime-tree, and so it is also known as the linden tree.

In the wild the small-leaved lime develops into a magnificent tree of 10–30m (30–100ft) in height. The tree has a very short trunk and with age a broadly spreading crown consisting of several similarly sized main boughs from which side branches grow horizontally. The buds grow alternately; they are mainly oval, pointed and somewhat indented at the sides. The side towards the sun is reddish-brown while the side away from the sun is yellow to olive green. The relatively small, heart-shaped leaves appear in late spring; in the autumn they turn bright yellow.

The hermaphrodite, yellowy-white flowers appear in early to midsummer and are an important food source for bees. The fruit, nuts almost as big as peas, have a leaf that serves as a wing for wind-powered distribution.

The small-leaved lime grows naturally in different woods and forests. It is also often planted along wide streets or singly in parks or open spaces.

Right: **Small-leaved lime in summer, about 50cm (20in) high and twelve years old, styled from a bought bonsai**

Far right: **Small-leaved lime in autumn, around 30cm (1ft) high, age twelve years, styled from a young plant**

Above left: **Lime flowers appear in the summer**

Above right: **The shoots of a lime can be recognised by the five-lobed leaves**

As bonsai

The small-leaved lime likes a sunny position in the wild but as a bonsai it should be kept in partial shade because of its sensitivity to excess minerals: in direct sunlight, evaporation causes mineral salts to accumulate in the soil and these leave behind so-called salt damage, which is visible in the most minor cases by brown edges on the leaves. If possible, use rainwater, especially in the height of summer, as this contains hardly any mineral salts and thus prevents a build up in the leaves. The lime can be kept damp but not waterlogged.

The soil should consist of one third peat, two thirds Japanese granules (*Akadama*) and some sand but other mixtures are also acceptable. Young plants need their soil changing every two years in the spring and the roots can be pruned at the same time.

For the most satisfactory development you need to feed the plant well. The small-leaved lime should be fed mainly with organic fertiliser. Additional mineral fertiliser is beneficial when its nutrient requirements are great, such as when the shoots appear in the spring or when bad weather means the nutrients are not released properly from the organic fertiliser. From late summer to early autumn the lime needs to be prepared for the winter with fertiliser that is high in potassium and low in nitrates.

The tree is overwintered either in the garden in a shady spot with the rootball planted in the soil without the container, or on a balcony in a box filled with peat and sand. In temperatures below −10°C (14°F) it should be covered with foil, leaves or twigs.

Cultivation

The small-leaved lime is easy to train, even the older branches can be bent. The broom is the Japanese style nearest to its natural habit, but the upright style is often chosen. All the styles are possible.

The best time for preliminary shaping of a new tree is between the time the buds swell up in the spring and the last four weeks of summer.

Pruning

The small-leaved lime accepts cutting well and will put forth shoots again within three weeks of each pruning. It can be made to produce shoots three to five times a year, if it is properly fed.

Stop pruning at the latest at the end of summer, and nip back any further growth so that the plant stops growing well before winter.

Larger branches should be removed in spring or during the main period of growth because at this time wounds seal particularly fast. Larger cuts should be sealed with a wound sealant.

A healthy small-leaved lime is amenable to leaf-cutting in early summer; this will significantly improve leaf size and twig structure.

Wiring

If you want to shape the tree using wire, the growth period is the best time to attach it. It must be done very carefully as the bark is very sensitive and wounds remain visible for a long time. Older branches are often easy to wire but particularly thick branches should be trained with anchoring wires.

Wires attached in the spring will become too tight by early summer and should be removed and new ones attached if necessary.

Propagation

Collect seeds towards the middle of autumn, keep them over the winter in damp sand in the fridge and sow them in the spring. They will often only germinate in the second year.

You can save a lot of time by starting off with a young plant instead of seeds.

In bonsai nurseries you will only find suitable young plants between two and five years old. Limes are sold in plant nurseries as well but are unsuitable for bonsai because they have long trunks. You will seldom find suitable plants in the wild.

Pests

The lime spider mite (*Eotetranychus telarius*) can be recognised by dirty brown coloration of the leaves, which then drop. It should be controlled with a special substance for spider mites as the plant is badly damaged by a severe attack. The spider mites overwinter in dropped leaves and in the upper levels of the soil, so you should remove all the leaves in the autumn as a preventive measure. If spider mite infestation reappears regularly, renew a large part of the soil every spring.

The larvae of the lime leaf wasp, which look like slugs, eat holes through the lower part of the leaves and leave the upper cell layer which then turns brown. Lime leaf wasp is controlled by collecting the dropped leaves.

Fungal diseases

Leaf spot in the lime is recognisable by yellow and then brown patches appearing even on young leaves and it is spread by spraying water.

These black spots, which often appear, are treated in the same way as leaf spot

The fungus can be prevented by applying a leaf spot fungicide in the spring.

Bark spot disease is characterised by reddish patches on the bark; these later turn black. The fungus can kill whole branches and should therefore be treated several times with fungicide.

Left: **Small-leaved lime in winter**

Smooth-leaved elm

(Ulmus carpinifolia)

This beautiful tree is becoming increasingly rare. 'Dutch elm disease', caused by fungi and transmitted by the elm sapwood beetle, has decimated native elms for years.

When grown as a bonsai the smooth-leaved elm is usually not endangered by Dutch elm disease, which is a good reason to keep it as a bonsai more often. In the wild, the smooth-leaved elm is found mainly as a shrub or a relatively small tree. This is most likely because the older trees have died off. It can grow to be several hundred years old and reach a height of up to 30m (100ft). In the open it develops a round, spreading leaf canopy with thick foliage and flat edges. The trunk is relatively short, and the bark, which is flat at first, splits open lengthways and develops raised rectangular patterns with age. The hermaphrodite greenish flowers, which are inconspicuous, appear in bunches from early to mid-spring before the leaves grow. After pollination, which is usually by the wind, round nuts with broad wings develop. These are already ripe in late spring and are wind distributed to germinate in the summer of the same year.

The alternate leaves, which are pointed, oval and asymmetrical, appear in late spring. In the autumn they turn bright yellow.

In Ulmus *carpinifolia* var. *suberosa* (Cork field elm), the young, relatively thin twigs may carry strips of cork that are later shed.

In the wild the elm grows in mixed woods and meadows, but also on dry hillsides.

As bonsai

Although the leaves reach a length of 8–10cm (3–4in) in the wild, they can be reduced to little more than 2cm (¾in) long in the bonsai without having to do anything particularly special. This, along with its willingness to be shaped through pruning alone, makes the elm one of the best native trees for bonsai. It needs no particular

Right:
Smooth-leaved elm in winter, around 70cm (28in) high and twelve years old, cultivated from a pre-shaped bonsai plant

Far right:
Smooth-leaved elm in autumn

situation and develops just as well in full sun as it does in partial shade. Windy positions are also acceptable. If it is in full sun or in the wind then it will obviously need a lot of water.

The elm likes limy soil so you can water it with hard tap water. It can be kept relatively damp. However, waterlogging should be avoided, as with most trees.

A tried and tested growing medium is a mix of loam granules (*Akadama*), sand and peat in proportions of 1:1:1 by weight. Other mixture proportions are also quite acceptable. The soil should be changed at least every two years, with both young and old trees.

The elm has high nutritional needs, so regular feeding is important. During the main period of growth you will get good results with either organic powder fertiliser or pellet fertiliser. Prepare the tree for autumn by using a mineral fertiliser that is rich in potassium in late summer.

Overwinter the bonsai elm in the garden, placing the rootball in the earth without its container, or on a balcony in a box filled with peat and sand. In temperatures of −5°C (23°F) and lower it should be additionally covered with foil, leaves or fir twigs.

Cultivation

The broom is the nearest to its natural habit. Most of the other Japanese styles are also possible – the double- and multiple-trunk styles being particularly striking.

Pruning

If the tree has recently been shaped give it a good start to the year by allowing its first spring shoots to grow quite long: about 20cm (8in) for young trees and 15cm (6in) for old trees. Prune it back well at this point.

The new shoots will appear after about two weeks, and can be cut back when they are 10cm (4in) long. This treatment ensures that the outer branches remain thin, and so the twig structure becomes particularly delicate. New shoots follow on after every pruning. At the end of summer pinch them out – removing the tip of the shoot as soon as a shoot has developed three or four leaves – so that the tree stops growing.

Older branches are best removed in the spring before the first shoots appear. Wound sealant must be applied carefully to the cuts.

Wiring

You can usually avoid using wires on the smooth-leaved elm, because the direction of growth is easily changed by selective pruning. When cultivating older plants it may be necessary to change the position of the branches and anchorage wires are useful.

Propagation

Collect seeds in late spring and sow them immediately. You might be lucky to find relatively young plants while out walking. If you collect a plant like this from the wild, it should be cultivated in the open garden for a further two to three years. While in the garden it can be shaped, but it should not be put into a container until the third year. This is the best way to get a powerful trunk; the delicate twig structure will develop in the container.

Very good plants to start bonsai are available in specialist bonsai nurseries. The full range of sizes and ages can be found.

Pests

The most common pests are various aphids.

The elm blister aphid causes the formation of big, blistery galls on the upper side of the leaves through sap sucking. Control it by cutting off the affected leaves.

The pear blood aphid (*Schizoneura anuginosa*) is found in big blisters, which are actually several leaves that have been distorted on young shoots. The insect itself is black but covered in a white waxy powder. The eggs are laid on the elm in the winter, and do not hatch until the spring. This insect is also easily controlled by cutting off affected parts.

The green elm roll leaf aphid (*Schizoneura ulmi*) is found in the rolled up edges of leaves. They can be successfully controlled with a suitable pesticide.

Apart from aphids the elm is also often affected by spider mites. They are not always easy to recognise as they are very small. Often, the most obvious clue is small white dots, their old skins, which can be seen under the leaves. Spider mites cause irregular grey streaks on the leaves; later the leaves fall off even if they are quite young. If spider mites are not kept under control, the plant is in danger of being killed.

Left: The elm's fruits have already ripened by the time the first leaves appear

Far left: Smooth-leaved elm, about 60cm (2ft) tall and twelve years old, pictured in the spring. It has been cultivated from a bought bonsai

Common juniper
(Juniperus communis)

Right: **Common
juniper, around
80cm (32in) high,
cultivated from a
wild seedling.**
*Designer: Werner
Trachsel*

Juniper is a very adaptable evergreen, occurring as a shrub and tree in various forms, from narrow, upright to spreading. In the wild common juniper is most often found on high moorlands where there is not too much competition from other trees. It is also common in sparse woods of both deciduous and coniferous trees.

It has grey-brown bark which peels off the trunk in threads, and needle-shaped leaves borne in triple whorls on the branches. The upper sides of the yellow-green leaves have single, broad blue-white stripes.

Juniper is dioecious. Male plants produce many flowers in small, round catkins; female flowers are carried individually and, once pollinated by the wind, take two years to develop into blue berries in the autumn of the second year.

As bonsai

The juniper needs a sunny, airy position to grow into a thick pin-cushion tree. Branches that are deprived of sunlight die or shrivel up.

Juniper can be watered all year round with tap water. In warm weather it is happiest in soil that is evenly damp but it will tolerate short periods of dryness if the roots are well developed.

Feed young plants well using organic fertiliser. Older, well-developed trees do not need so much food.

The common juniper is very hardy, but it is still better to plant it

out in the garden without its container over the winter so that the soil remains evenly damp throughout the cold weather.

Cultivation

The basic shaping is best undertaken between mid-spring and the end of summer.

The common juniper is very

similar to the Japanese juniper so the form of the Japanese juniper can be used as inspiration for its training and shaping. Taking its natural habit as a pattern is not very exciting.

Pruning

Allow seedlings to grow without cutting back for the first three years. In older plants, when the shoots are 2–3cm (¾–1¼in) long cut them back by a third, by nipping off the end of the shoot to retain thick needles. To get thicker branches, leave the leading shoot undisturbed but cut back any other new shoots on the branch. This will give you thick needles along with strong thickening growth.

Larger cuts recover very slowly; they heal most quickly if they are made in spring and treated immediately with sealant.

Wiring

Two-year-old branches are the most easy to wire as they are strong but not yet too thick or stiff. Wiring is effective, as thickening is not pronounced and the bark is not overly sensitive and gradually peels off. Carry out training in the growing period and keep the tree in the shade for a few days afterwards.

Propagation

Collect berries in the autumn and keep the seeds over the winter in damp sand in the fridge. Sow them in spring. Many of the seeds will not germinate until the second year.

Juniper is easily propagated by cuttings taken in summer; root hormone produces good results.

While you will rarely find the wild form of the juniper in nurseries and specialist bonsai nurseries you are likely to find many different cultivars.

Wild specimens that are suitable for bonsai are not common. Even if you do find a good one they tend to have small and compact root systems which cause difficulty when digging up. If you do have the opportunity to dig up a wild juniper, you should not do so before taking the advice of a specialist, who will need to know the exact conditions under which you plan to cultivate the tree. It will have the greatest chances of survival if it is collected in spring before the shoots appear

Pests

Greeny-yellow needles are a sign of an attack of spider mites. The conifer spinning mite (*Olygonichus ununguis*) later causes a pale grey-green coloration which then turns reddish-brown. A bad attack will produce numerous threads of web on the tips of the shoots. The plant should be treated with a spray for spider mites.

Scale insects may also attack the juniper. They are relatively conspicuous and light grey in colour, and occur in large numbers and may greatly hinder the tree's development. The best way to control them is to kill them at the

crawler stage with non-persistent contact insecticides or use systemic insecticide, which may damage the plant.

The pine needle caterpillar (*Archips piceana*) forms webs and eats the needles. Collect and destroy the caterpillars or remove and destroy the affected parts of the tree.

Fungal diseases

Young shoots changing colour from yellow to brown and eventually dying are a sign of fungal disease. The affected twigs become brittle, and the bark can clearly be seen to be dying off. Control the fungus by cutting back the affected parts of the plant and spraying several times with an appropriate fungicide.

Rust fungus is apparent through tongue-shaped, bright orange growths on branches which then die. Hawthorn rust, rowan rust and pear rust also affect the juniper. Affected plants are usually unusable for bonsai cultivation and should be destroyed. You can try to save valuable trees by cutting off the affected parts of the plant and spraying with a rust fungus spray, or try Bordeaux mixture. To prevent rust from occurring it is wise to ensure that any potential host trees (which may include some you are growing as bonsai) stay free of it in the first place.

European larch

(Larix decidua)

The larch is deciduous; it is the only conifer in central Europe whose leaves change colour in autumn. It is native to mountainous areas in Europe but is just as often found in flat regions, as it is widely used in forestry.

Under normal circumstances the tree grows to 25–30m (80–100ft) in height and has a conical silhouette. Young shoots are a yellowy-brown colour and as it gets older the trunk and sickle-shaped branches develop rough bark.

The needles form from mid- to late spring and are clustered together in groups. Some of the clusters sprout long shoots, on which the needles grow singly. Other clusters stop growing and form only short shoots; there are many of these on the older branches.

The larch is monoecious and from wind-pollinated, reddish female flowers it bears relatively small, oval cones which sit on the branches,. The cones open in mid-autumn, allowing the winged seeds to be dispersed by the wind.

As bonsai

The larch is easy to keep as a bonsai. It likes a sunny position, but can also be kept in partial shade. It should be kept damp throughout the year; in very hot weather it will only be prevented from dropping its needles if the soil is kept properly damp. If the weather is predominantly cool, it can tolerate short periods of dryness without coming to any harm.

Right: **A larch wood just as the leaves are beginning to turn.** *Designer: Hermann Pieper*

Larches need a loose, grainy growing medium. A good mix is loam granules (*Akadama*) and lava granules in proportions of 2:1. Other mixtures such as loam, sand and peat in relative weights of 2:2:1 are also suitable. Young plants need the soil changing every two years, older cultivated bonsai every three to five years. The roots can be pruned at the same time.

Young plants need to be well fed: this produces faster trunk thickening and branching but, unfortunately, it also makes the needles grow very long. Older, well-developed bonsai that have already formed bark need only be given small amounts of fertiliser. In any case the length of the shoots can be kept down and the size of the needles kept small by giving a low nitrogen fertiliser.

The larch is very hardy but in

order to ensure an even dampness in the soil during the cold months, it should be planted in the garden without its container over the winter.

Cultivation

The larch can be trained in many different styles, most of which are also found in the wild. Cultivating older plants is not difficult as branches remain easy to bend for several years. The best time for the basic shaping of a new plant or a wild sapling is between late spring and midsummer.

Pruning

When the spring shoots are about 5cm (2in) long, you will be able to see the next generation of buds ready to sprout. You can establish the direction of these shoots at this stage; the last bud on the shoot after pruning will produce new shoots so make sure it is pointing in the right direction. The longer you wait before pruning, the stronger the branch will become. A young plant should be left until the shoots are 10–20cm (4–8in) long in order to achieve a strong basic branch framework, but older trees can be trimmed sooner.

Depending on whether you want a branch to be longer or not, you can cut the shoots back moderately or hard. If the twig structure becomes too thick, whole new shoots can be removed down to the old wood; this often happens at the top of the tree. In older trees where most of the shaping work has already been done, the new shoots can be nipped back or pulled off. Remove the tip with tweezers or your fingertips when the shoot is 2–3cm ($\frac{3}{4}$–$1\frac{1}{4}$in) long. This will produce particularly delicate, thin twig networks in the outer part of the leaf covering.

Wiring

Older branches are easily bent but avoid using wires on young branches where the bark is about to develop otherwise you may cause damage. These branches are better anchored.

The best time to wire larches is in the spring, when the buds are just turning green and about to open. During this time there are no needles in the way, and the branches are so full of sap that it is impossible to kill them by drastically changing their direction of growth. Six weeks after the first shoots appear, the wires may already be too tight, and should be renewed carefully.

Propagation

Collect seeds in the autumn, keep them in a dry place and sow them in the spring.

Plants that are two to five years old can be found in the usual tree nurseries. You will also find them in specialist bonsai nurseries where they will have already been cut

back several times, so when you are shaping them you will not have to make any drastic cuts.

In some habitats you may find very old larches which have remained small. They can be very gnarled and look almost comical but you must resist the temptation to take them home for bonsai cultivation as such trees, dug up by a lay person, have little chance of survival. Leave them where they are – for conservation considerations as much as anything else.

In mountainous areas, for example, even the smaller peripheral trees have an important role to play in holding the soil together and preventing erosion. This naturally alpine tree is also widely grown in the British Isles for its strong timber, however, and is often found in mixed forests. Young saplings have the greatest chance of survival if they are gathered between autumn and spring, but always remember to get permission before digging up a tree and bear in mind the Japanese legend which says that for each tree taken from the wild another should be planted in its place.

Pests

The larch woolly aphid (*Adelges laricis*) is relatively common and easy to recognise by its furry excretions; it can also be spotted by the brownish colour of the places where it has sucked sap and the bent needles. During its development it may change hosts using the spruce as an intermediary. Spray affected plants thoroughly with HCH or malathion.

The larvae of a small dark insect (*Taeniothrips laricivorus*) suck sap and cause larch blister foot, where the plant suffers atrophy and the tips of the shoots die off. Control an attack with a contact insecticide, such as HCH or malathion.

The larvae of the larch leaf miner (*Coleophora laricella*) live off the insides of the larch needles, the tips of which become transparent. It is easy to control by removing the affected shoots.

Fungal diseases

Larch needle drop makes the older needles on the shoots turn unevenly brown and then fall off. It can lead to the whole tree dying. Control it with applications of Bordeaux mixture.

Right: Larch cone

Far right: European larch, about 50cm (20in) high and twenty-five years old, cultivated from a seedling. *Designer: Hans Kastner*

Norway spruce

(Picea abies)

The evergreen Norway spruce, also called the common or red spruce, occurs in the wild in mixed woodland areas in the mountainous regions of Europe. It is also found on the edges of high moorland and meadows and is often planted for forestry use. Norway spruce has many cultivated varieties and it is these that are most often found in gardens or even graveyards.

The tree is conical in habit with a pointed top and branches that begin close to the ground. With age it develops a flat, flaky bark. Under normal circumstances it grows to 25–40m (80–130ft) high, but taller trees have been known. The branches are strong and bark-covered and droop downwards. In the mountainous regions this drooping is quite steep, caused by a frequent burden of snow.

The male flowers are borne together in catkins and are red, turning yellow as they ripen. The female flowers look like red 'candles' and after pollination by the wind they develop into pendent brown spruce cones which release their winged fruit in the autumn.

This evergreen tree puts forth new shoots in late spring. Each needle sits on a small raised nodule and they grow all around the shoot. They also occur individually growing directly out of some branches, particularly on the side facing the sun. In its high mountainous habitat the needles remain extremely short.

As bonsai

The Norway spruce bonsai prefers a partially shaded position that is airy but also protected from strong wind to prevent damage from drying out. The Norway spruce suffers from sunburn if it is taken out of the shade and put in the sun, or if the side turned away from the sun is suddenly turned

Right: A Norway spruce of about 90cm (3ft) high, cultivated from a wild seedling.
Designer: Walter Pall

towards it. Remember this when taking the tree out of its winter quarters.

It is sensitive to mineral salts so is best given rainwater. If this is not available, it should be watered generously so that a large part of the water can drain off through the bottom of the container, washing away much of the potentially damaging salts.

The Norway spruce should always be kept damp but at the same time it should not be waterlogged. To avoid this use a porous soil and renew it every two years: a mix of loam granules, sand and peat in proportions of 2:1:1 in weight is ideal, as are other porous growing mixtures.

Young plants need a generous dose of organic bonsai fertiliser from when the shoots appear until early autumn. Older, well-developed bonsai that you want to develop shorter needles can manage on very small amounts of fertiliser, or even a whole year without any. This ensures that growth and thickening are radically reduced.

The spruce is very hardy, but to ensure that the roots remain evenly moist throughout the winter months it should be planted out in the garden without its container, or in a box filled with a mixture of peat and sand.

Norway spruce is very sensitive to late frosts in the spring, and should therefore be protected from frost as soon as the first shoots begin to develop.

Cultivation

All the Japanese styles are suitable for the spruce, including the broom style. Under optimum conditions its natural habit is nearest to the upright style.

Norway spruce

Left: **Norway spruce, around 90cm (36in) high, cultivated from a wild specimen.** *Designer: Werner Trachsel*

109

Pruning

Older branches may be removed in winter. On well-developed branches, new shoots are reduced by half when they are 2–3cm ($\frac{3}{4}$–1$\frac{1}{4}$in) long. Twist the piece you want to remove between two fingers or snap it off with your fingernails. If you want the branches to grow stronger, remove only the main shoots.

Wiring

Thickening is quite slow, so spruces can be wired without danger of permanent scarring as long as they are carefully looked after. Older branches often need several years of training before they grow in the right direction. If the wire becomes too tight in the meantime, it should be removed and replaced.

Propagation

Collect seeds in the autumn, store them in a dry place and sow them in the spring.

Spruces can be found in any tree nursery and at Christmas they are available on almost every street corner at a variety of different ages. In specialist bonsai nurseries they are less common, and young plants are often impossible to find.

Spruce can grow in quite adverse conditions, between rocks in crevices for example, so you may come across very ancient ones which have remained small as a result, but these must not be dug up. Old spruces are in any case very difficult to repot successfully; it gets even more difficult with ancient trees that have anchored their branching roots deep into rocks and can only be dug up if these are broken. Very occasionally a plant might survive this sort of treatment, but this cannot justify the death of many others.

If digging it up is the only chance of survival for the plant, you will be more likely to be successful in resettling the tree between early autumn and the spring.

As a bonsai, a high mountain spruce will develop very short needles if it is looked after near where it was found but if it is brought down to lower altitudes, the needles will grow longer. It has been said that if a spruce bonsai is cultivated at a height of over 600m (1800ft), it will develop short needles of its own accord, and in lower areas it will develop longer ones.

You may also find interesting spruces outside mountainous areas. As already mentioned, you should always obtain the permission of the relevant forestry authorities before removing them.

In mountainous areas the spruce develops very short needles on its shoots

Pests

The conifer spinning mite is characterised by yellowy-green spots on the needles and the threads in between them. The needles later turn brown. It can be controlled with a spray for spider mites.

The sitka spruce aphid *(Elatobium abietinum)* is a small green insect with red eyes which sucks the tree's sap, causing needles that are attacked to drop off. The safest way to prevent it is by spraying the new shoots with a tar oil. In the case of an attack, it should be treated quickly with malathion.

The larvae of the common spruce needle wasp (*Cephaleia abietis*) eat the older spruce needles, protected by nests in the forks of the branches. Remove the larvae from the tree along with the whole nest.

The larvae of the spruce nest weaver (*Epitnotia tedella*) hollow out the needles from the base. Their nests, which consist of several needles woven together are easy to spot. If there is only one of them it is often sufficient to simply remove the affected needles or shoots but in a bad case it may be necessary to spray the tree for mining larvae.

The white woolly spruce trunk aphid is easy to recognise by its fluffy white secretions, under which it hides, draining the sap. It can destroy whole branches so should be treated several times with a non-toxic spray containing a few drops of washing-up liquid as soon as it appears.

Pineapple-shaped swellings of the tips of the shoots are caused by various spruce gall mites. These can easily be controlled by removing and destroying the galls.

Left: The bark of an old spruce bonsai

Far left: Spruce, around 40cm (16in) high, cultivated from a wild seedling
Designer: Walter Pall

111

Arolla pine or Swiss stone pine

(Pinus cembra)

This slow-growing mountain tree often has a very irregular, low-branched, conical leaf canopy in the wild. At 5–12cm (2–5in) long its needles are the longest of all the native pines and are usually blunt. They are grouped in fives, so you can easily distinguish the Arolla pine from other native pines, which all have needles in pairs. The Weymouth pine (*Pinus strobus*) also has five needles and is quite often found in forestry plantations, but it has thinly pointed needles and winged fruit.

The bark, which is silvery grey and smooth at first, turns dark reddish-brown and rough with age.

The flowers appear as the tree gets older: the males are in reddish catkins, the females in violet cones. The fruits – unwinged pine nuts – are edible.

As bonsai

The Arolla pine likes a sunny position, but will tolerate partial shade, and does not need protection from wind.

The growing medium should be very porous and can consist of a mixture of fine gravel, loam granules and crushed lava. For young plants it should be changed at least every two years; if the soil is changed less often, the needles will grow shorter, but the tree will also grow much more slowly.

Arolla pine does not need much in the way of nutrients, but generous fertilising helps faster growth, which means you get the shape you want more quickly. It needs no protection in winter.

Cultivation

Due to its very long needles and thick branches, the Arolla pine is very rarely kept as a bonsai. You can only achieve a really distinctive shape with larger bonsai, as the contours of smaller trees are shrouded by the pine's long needles. All the Japanese forms, including the broom style, are suitable and the formal or informal upright style are easy to obtain. You can train a well-rooted, bought plant the whole year round.

Wiring

Older main branches should be wired at the first shaping; the relatively thick twigs can be bent for a long time and are easily wired. The needles should, of course, be removed where the wire runs along.

Pruning

If the current year's young branches are cut back or removed completely in midsummer, new buds develop. These can produce shoots in the same year and will then grow shorter needles.

Thicker branches are removed in winter, when the tree will not secrete so much resin.

Propagation

Collect seeds when they are ripe, store them in a dry place and sow them in the spring.

Suitable wild specimens are rare.

Specialist bonsai nurseries hardly ever stock this tree so the search for suitable bonsai material is limited to tree nurseries, which often have the Arolla pine in a range of ages.

Below: **Compared with the mountain pine, the shoots of the Arolla pine are very thick so fine branching is very difficult to achieve**

112

Left: Arolla pine, around 50cm (20in) high. *Designer: Walter Pall*

Mountain pine

(Pinus mugo)

Far right: **Mountain pine, around 90cm (3ft) high, cultivated from a wild sapling**

Below: **Mountain pine, around 90cm (3ft) high.** *Designer:* **Walter Pall**

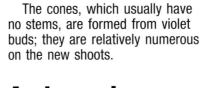

The mountain pine occurs both as a tree and as a shrub. In the young tree the bark is a shiny green to violet colour, becoming rough and grey-brown to black with age. The buds are resiny; the needles are carried in pairs, are 2–5cm (¾–2in) long depending on their position and they can live for up to ten years. They are slightly twisted and uniformly green.

The cones, which usually have no stems, are formed from violet buds; they are relatively numerous on the new shoots.

As bonsai

You should select a sunny position which receives hardly any wind: branches that are constantly in the shade wither and even die.

Mountain pines should be kept constantly damp, but may tolerate dryness for a short time. They can be given hard tap water as well as rainwater.

There are no particular requirements as far as the soil is concerned; it can be very sandy or loamy, but grainy soil encourages root growth. A mix of *Akadama*, fine gravel and lava granules, used in proportions of 2:1:1, is quite acceptable. The soil needs changing every three years for trees which have already been shaped.

The length of the needles is governed by the nutrients available to the tree: the higher the nitrogen content of the fertiliser, the longer the needles grow. While the tree is young, the shape and thickness of the trunk and good branching are all more important than the length of the needles so the tree should be fed generously from mid-spring to late summer. Rapeseed pellets or other solid organic fertilisers can be used and you can also give it mineral fertiliser all year round.

The mountain pine can live symbiotically with *mycorrhiza* fungus. This whitish-grey fungus is easy to spot when the rootball is taken out of the container and its presence usually makes the tree healthier and more robust.

Mountain pines are very frost hardy, but should be planted in the garden without the container to ensure an even dampness of the soil over the winter.

Cultivation

The mountain pine can be shaped into many styles and is one of the most commonly cultivated species of native pines. Literati and cascade forms are very popular at exhibitions.

Wiring

Older branches are usually easy to wire, but should be anchored if the bark has already grown. The mountain pine can be wired in the winter or during the growing season. Wires attached in the spring may be too tight by the summer and will grow inwards in the autumn if not removed.

Pruning

Trees that have not recently been collected from the wild, and are healthy and have a good root system, can be cut back into the old wood at the first shaping in the summer as long as there are still some green needles on the remaining part of the branch. These branches produce more resin than those that have been cut in winter, but they put forth lots of new buds after about four weeks — not only at the wound but also along the whole branch.

With trees that have already been shaped, the spring shoots should be cut back in midsummer or removed completely. If the spring growth was very weak, you can nip off the bud at the end of every shoot. After about four weeks, new buds will develop on the wound and also on areas of the branch that receive a lot of sun. These will put forth again in the same year if they are well fed, remain short and develop smaller needles. Strong branches are removed in winter.

Propagation

Collect seeds when they are ripe, keep them dry and sow them in the spring.

Mountain pines of many ages and forms can be found in plant nurseries and specialist bonsai nurseries. They are usually grown as shrubs but can be shaped into individual trees as well.

Wild specimens are collected in the spring before the buds start to swell but remember to obtain permission before digging them up. Unlike deciduous trees, pine branches that are cut back when the tree is collected usually die off, so only branches that are not needed for cultivation should be cut back at this stage. The plant should then be kept for at least a year in a larger container or in the open garden, without being cut back. After this you can gradually, year by year, cut back the overhanging branches, until you have a compact bonsai that is ready to be shaped.

Austrian pine

(Pinus nigra)

The Austrian pine, another double-needled pine, can be distinguished by its very strong, relatively long, dark green needles, which remain on the tree for four to five years, and its bark which roughens with age.

In the wild the crown is initially oval to round, becoming umbrella-shaped with age.

The structure of the flowers is similar to that of other pines. The male catkins, which grow up to 2½cm (1in) long, are golden yellow and borne in groups. The female flowers are cone-shaped, reddish and are produced either singly or in pairs. The tree is wind-pollinated.

All parts of the Austrian pine are stronger than the Scots pine (p.118), its shoots usually remain shorter and are more stocky.

As bonsai

Choose as sunny a site as possible, branches that are deprived of sunlight will die, but the Austrian pine can withstand a windy position.

For soil use a mix of Japanese loam granules (*Akadama*), peat and coarse sand in proportions of 2:1:1 by weight. It is important that the soil is porous and for plants that are developing it should be changed every two years. This can be done in late summer, so that new roots form by winter.

Keep the soil moist because the Austrian pine, like other pines, lives symbiotically with a soil fungus, which helps it to draw water and makes nutrients easily available to

Far right: **Austrian pine shortly after shaping**

it. The fungus disappears if the soil becomes waterlogged. You can use hard tap water.

Begin feeding the plant when the buds begin to show in spring. Younger trees need more feeding than older ones; nutrients can be given in organic or mineral form.

Overwinter it in the garden, with the rootball planted in a light but shady place. On a balcony the tree can be overwintered with the rootball in a box filled with a mixture of peat and sand.

Cultivation

Because of its strong growth and long needles, you should aim for a height of at least 50cm (20in). All Japanese styles are attainable.

Pruning

The first shaping is carried out in the summer, when the branches of healthy, well-rooted and well-fed trees can be cut back so there are only a few needles remaining, if necessary. Within a few weeks numerous new buds develop all over the branches.

With trees that have just been shaped, remove the large end buds either before or while they are swelling. These will have developed mainly in the top third of the leaf covering. The shoots that develop after this are shorter, and the formation of new side branches is encouraged.

In midsummer you can remove this new growth again as it will

now have matured. It can be cut back either completely or by up to two thirds, depending on its position in the tree. Numerous buds will grow from the cuts and some will also appear on the old wood. These buds may develop again in the same year but if they become too long they can be shortened again.

Wiring

Unlike the mountain pine or the Scots pine the older branches of the Austrian pine are not easy to wire. They are better anchored to prevent damage to the bark.

Branches up to three years old can be wired as long as the needles are removed from where the wire is to run.

Trees that have been in a bonsai container for a while are wired in winter and during the growing period, while newly collected or repotted trees are better wired in the summer. Leave the wire on for a year at the longest.

Propagation

Collect seeds when they are ripe from autumn to early spring, keep them in a dry place and sow them in the spring.

Plants suitable for cultivation are rarely found in nurseries, nor are they common in specialist bonsai centres. You may occasionally find roughly-shaped trees.

Wild seedlings are very seldom suitable for bonsai cultivation.

Scots pine

(Pinus sylvestris)

Scots pine is an evergreen forest tree and is found in many different shapes, although mature specimens usually develop an irregular conical or umbrella-shaped silhouette. The dark, deeply-fissured, rough trunk goes right to the top of the tree. The bark of the younger parts of the tree is often orangey-red and comes off in paper-thin flakes.

The needles are in pairs and grow to 3–8cm (1¼–3in) long depending on their position on the tree. They are often twisted once between the base and the tip. In the summer they are blue-green to grey-green. The sides curve inwards and the outer side is a slightly different colour to the inner.

Male flowers appear as yellow catkins; female flowers are round and red. They are wind pollinated and develop into stemmed pendent cones containing winged fruits, which ripen in the autumn of the second year and are distributed by the wind.

As bonsai

The Scots pine needs a sunny position and can be watered copiously with tap water. It is hardy and does not need to be protected from frost.

Soil can be a mix of loam granules and fine gravel in proportions of 2:1 but other mixtures have also been successful.

The length of the needles increases with the moisture of the soil and with the level of nutrients.

Young plants need more feeding than older trees.

Cultivation

All the Japanese and other styles can be used, although the broom style is unusual. Wild seedlings or newly bought plants that have well-developed roots can be given their first shaping at any time of the year but if you do this in winter, you must protect the plant from frost.

Pruning

'Candles' that have grown longer than 3–4cm (1¼–1½in) by the end of spring are removed completely. New buds develop where they were removed; these in turn become candles and then short shoots. From midsummer, if they have hardened a little, they can be cut back along with the shoots which have been left untouched up until this point. New buds continue to develop at the cuts until winter, and will produce needles the following spring.

Wiring

Wiring cannot be avoided if you want to keep a Scots pine in shape. Well-rooted pine bonsai should be wired up to the tips of their branches at least every two years. This is best done in winter, with every side branch and every twig positioned so that none

obscures another, this ensures that thick cushions of needles will develop. The wire must be removed during the course of the following year, well before it starts to grow in.

Propagation

Collect seeds from autumn until early spring. Store them in a dry place and sow them in the spring.

Young plants and bonsai that have already been cultivated are seldom found in specialist nurseries but bonsai which have had one basic shaping are becoming more widely available.

Sometimes you will find suitable plants in the wild: obtain permission before you dig them up.

Pests

The pine gall midge (*Thecodiplosis brachyntera*) makes individual pairs of needles turn yellow. Their bases merge and thicken into a blister in which the midge larvae eat and pupate. You can pluck off and destroy individual pairs of needles. In a bad case, they must be treated with a special spray (ask in a garden centre).

The pine twig aphid (*Cinara pini*), a large, black, sap-sucking aphid, causes its main damage by the formation of rust on its sticky secretions. Pests occurring singly can be driven off with a jet of water but a stubborn attack calls for a contact insecticide, such as malathion.

The caterpillars of various pine shoot-wrapping moths (*Rhyacionia* spp.) kill the tips of the shoots or make them grow crooked by eating the buds and the new shoots. Affected tips of shoots are removed and destroyed.

The various pine woolly aphids are easy to recognise by their woolly white secretions and they weaken the plant by draining its sap. A bad case can kill it. Control the aphids by spraying several times with a non-toxic spray for sap-sucking insects that also contains some detergent.

Fungal diseases

Pine needle drop first appears as small brown spots on the needles. These become more and more obvious from autumn until spring and make the whole needle die and drop from the tree in late spring. The current year's shoots are not affected by it but a new infection can follow in summer from the fallen needles. All fallen needles should be removed and destroyed. In the summer, during the period of infection, treat the plant several times with a suitable spray such as Bordeaux mixture.

Shoot disease makes the buds go dry and the needles on year-old shoots begin to go yellow from the base upwards. Eventually shoot disease can kill the whole tree. You need a specialist to help you diagnose and control this disease.

Pine bark blister rust is characterised by blistery, oval, yellowy tumours, which protrude from the bark. After a few days they burst, freeing the yellow spores. The blisters reoccur year after year and lead to the affected shoot dying off. There are two types of blister rust, one that changes its host and one that remains with the same host. Cut off and destroy affected branches.

Twisting rust causes the shoots to grow in an s-shape. The bark splits open in early summer revealing the yellow spores of the fungus. If there is no re-infection, the fungus only remains with the tree for a year. It alternates its host tree with the poplar and you can control it by cutting off and destroying the affected parts of the plant.

Scots pine

Left: **Scots pine, around 20cm (8in) high, cultivated from a wild sapling.**
Designer: Walter Pall

Yew

(Taxus baccata)

This slow-growing evergreen conifer can live up to 1000 years old. This, and the fact that it has short needles, makes it especially suited for bonsai cultivation.

A young tree is frequently wider than it is tall and with age will often develop an oval silhouette that is more reminiscent of a deciduous tree. The yew typically produces several trunks or several tips.

The needles are carried singly and are shiny-green on top and pale green underneath. They are usually arranged in two rows opposite each other. The tree puts forth light to reddish-green shoots in mid-spring.

It is a dioecious plant, developing flowers while still quite young. The male flowers are borne in small, yellow catkins; the females are single, very small and inconspicuous, and look like a bud. The fruit is a red berry with edible, sweet, juicy flesh but all other parts of the plant, including the seed, are poisonous.

Right: **Yew berries and leaves**

Far right: **Yew tree, about 90cm (3ft) high, cultivated from nursery stock**

The bark of the trunk is flat and, as it flakes off in irregular pieces, varies from brown to reddish-brown. The tree's inner network of branches looks like cords of muscles from the base of the trunk upwards. In the wild it is always quite similar in appearance and there are a few cultivated varieties that may be found in parks and gardens.

As bonsai

Yew likes a sunny or shady position. In constant sunshine you will find it almost impossible to keep up with its need for water and in shade the shoots grow weakly, so a site in partial shade is the most preferable. It does not like strong wind, but will withstand it for a short time.

Yew can be watered with hard tap water, as long as you ensure that minerals do not build up in the soil. It cannot tolerate dryness, even for a short time, and reacts to lack of water by dropping its older needles. As a rule, if the rootball is dry, the whole tree will die at once.

The potting compost should contain little peat. A mix of loam granules (*Akadama*), sand and lava granules in proportions of 3:1:1 by weight has been proven to be suitable, but other medium- to coarse-grained mixtures that are not too rich in humus are also acceptable.

Feeding, with an organic solid bonsai fertiliser, should start when the new shoots appear and continue until late summer.

The tree is only semi-hardy and so should be well protected in winter. Overwinter it in the garden with the rootball planted in the soil, or on a balcony in a box filled with peat and sand.

In temperatures below −10°C (14°F) the tree should be covered with foil, straw or leaves.

Cultivation

Because yew grows so slowly it is advisable to use plants that are already several years old for shaping. There are many different options for shaping yew as it puts forth new shoots very happily from old wood and even an unshaped sapling will have a thick covering of needles near the trunk so it can be cut back hard without leaving it completely bare.

In the wild the tree will develop several tips so none of the Japanese styles resemble the yew's natural shape.

Older nursery trees can be shaped with great success and are therefore recommended.

Wiring

Young branches up to three years old are easy to wire but older branches should be anchored. The tree will keep its shape from very early on: one- to two-year-old shoots need only be wired for one growing period. Older branches usually retain their shape after two years wiring at the most. The new shoots appear mostly horizontally,

Right: **Yew, around 80cm (32in) high, cultivated from a nursery tree.** *Designer: Wolf D. Schudde*

so the tree should not need wiring again and again. It often requires only careful pruning to keep it in shape.

Pruning

Older branches can be removed at any time of year. Wounds heal very slowly, even when they are well sealed.

With younger plants that have still to develop, leave all the shoots on the side branches and cut back the shoots growing directly upwards. These grow in abundance as the yew tends to develop several tips.

Cut back the new shoots of older plants that have already been shaped by a third when they are 5–10cm (2–4in) long.

Propagation

Collect the fruit in summer when they are red, remove the seeds from the flesh and keep them in damp sand in the fridge until they are sown in spring.

Birds feed on the seeds so you will often find seedlings below their perches, for example near garden fences.

Young and older plants suitable for shaping are found in many nurseries and some specialist bonsai nurseries. Trees that have already been shaped are increasingly available.

Wild specimens suitable for bonsai are rare.

Pests

The yew bowl scale insect (*Eulecanium cornicrudum*) weakens the plant by sucking its sap, so the

Left: **Yew, around 70cm (28in) high, cultivated from a nursery tree.** *Designer: Gerhard Paschke*

shoots remain very weak. Sooty mould grows on the sticky excreta of the insect and damages the tree indirectly by blocking out the light. Control this pest with a spray for scale insects available from garden centres.

Weevils leave indents on the needles where they have eaten them away; their larvae eat the roots. These pests move very slowly so they are difficult to find. You should use an effective contact insecticide.

The bud gall mite (*Cecidophypsis psilaspis*) causes flower and shoot buds to become deformed, turning them into small galls a few millimetres across. Control the mites by removing and destroying the galls.

123

Arctic birch

(Betula nana)

The arctic birch is a moorland plant. At first glance there is no clue that this rare shrub is related to the silver-trunked birches. The dark branches are dotted with white and have roundish green leaves about 10mm (½in) long, which look more like those of a beech and turn bright yellow in autumn.

The plant is monoecious and produces leaves and flowers in late spring, often at the same time. The wind pollinates the flowers, which are borne together in small catkins. The fruit, which look like cones, also form close together, making upward-facing clusters.

As bonsai

The arctic birch needs a sunny position when grown as a bonsai, as in the shade branches will frequently die off. It does not like heat and reacts to extreme heat by shedding its leaves like other birches, so the position should also be airy. It should be kept moist

Right: **Multiple fruit of the Arctic birch**

and, as it likes acid soil, rainwater should be used. Even short periods of dryness will make it drop its leaves.

As a soil you can use a mix of loam, sand and peat in proportions of 1:1:2 by weight. Two-thirds of the soil should be changed every two years; the roots can be pruned at the same time and the tree should be fed moderately with organic pellet fertiliser. Overwinter it in the garden in a bright but not sunny position, planting the rootball in the soil without its container, or on a balcony in a box filled with peat and sand.

Cultivation

In nature the arctic birch only has a few interesting shapes but all the Japanese and other styles are suitable. Thickening is slow so you should keep the tree in the ground for a few years, until the basic structure is strong and only the delicate branching has to be developed.

Pruning

In younger plants the new spring shoots are cut back to between two and seven leaves when they are about 15cm (6in) long, depending on which shape you are aiming for.

Older plants that have just been shaped and already have well-developed trunks, can be cut back earlier or nipped back after the third leaf appears.

The arctic birch will happily put forth again after each pruning, often in as little as two weeks, so it needs trimming at least three times a year. Prune it for the last time towards the end of summer; growth will then stop because the tree has only been given a moderate amount of fertiliser.

Older branches are removed in the spring when the new leaves appear, or later up to the last month of summer.

Larger cuts should be sealed well, otherwise infections in the wound can easily lead to parts of the plant dying.

Wiring

Wire the tree in the spring when the leaves are just beginning to appear, as any damage to the tree's sap tissue at this stage will be repaired, and leaves are not yet in the way. The plant will also tolerate careful wiring from late spring to midsummer but branches wired in winter often die in spring, particularly if their direction is drastically altered.

Only branches up to two years old can be wired without leaving permanent scars and even these can put up so much resistance that the wire leaves behind pressure marks. So older branches should be trained in the desired direction using anchoring wires.

Arctic birch is slow to thicken so the wire can remain on the tree for the whole growing season or even for a year.

Left: Arctic birch, around 30cm (12in) high and ten years old, cultivated from a bonsai sapling. *Designer: Dieter Schmidt*

Propagation

The Arctic birch is a rare species and should never be taken from the wild, not even seed.

Young plants and older saplings as well as young bonsai which have just been shaped, are often found in specialist nurseries.

Pests

Unlike other birches, the arctic birch is often affected by spider mites, which can be recognised by yellowy-green spotted leaves. You can control it with a spray for spider mites. Pests that attack the silver birch can also affect the Arctic birch (see p.65). Birch rust is common with its yellow to orangey-red pustules on the underside of the leaves and can be prevented by fortnightly sprayings with Bordeaux mixture.

Hazel

(Coryllus avellana)

Hazel is often found in gardens and reaches a height of 5m (15ft). The grey-brown bark remains smooth as the tree gets older and the young shoots are hairy.

The monoecious flowers often appear in late winter, long before the leaves. The little, inconspicuous, bud-like, female flowers are only a few millimetres in size and grow in clusters. They have protruding red stigmas, which can only be seen from close up. The male flowers develop conspicuous yellow catkins, are wind-pollinated and later develop into the well-known edible hazelnuts.

The short-stemmed leaves which appear in mid-spring are broadly heart-shaped, pointed and hairy. In the autumn they turn yellow to orange.

Hazel shrubs are often found on the edges of woods and in the undergrowth, and grow like the oak, in many mixed woods. Red-leaved varieties occur in the wild and can be found in parks and gardens.

Right: **Hazel, around 60cm (2ft) high and ten years old, cultivated from a bonsai sapling**

As bonsai

It likes a sunny to partially shaded position. A sunny position is only suitable if the tree is given water that is low in minerals, as hazel is sensitive to high levels, which occur more frequently when the sun causes greater evaporation.

Windy places are not suitable as the tree will dry out too quickly. In places that are shady and protected from the wind, you can give it hard tap water.

There are no particular requirements as far as soil is concerned, so you can use a standard mix. Replace most of the soil every two to three years, cutting back the roots at the same time.

Feed your hazel from mid-spring until the latter part of summer with solid organic bonsai fertiliser.

Overwinter it with the rootball planted in the garden without a container, in a bright place protected from the sun, or on a balcony in a box filled with peat and sand.

Cultivation

The hazel can be shaped into all the Japanese and other styles. Basic shaping is undertaken with a new sapling between the buds swelling in the spring and midsummer.

Pruning

New buds are produced on the trunk after every pruning so if they are not needed they should be removed as soon as possible.

Older branches should be cut back when the leaves appear in spring or before the end of

summer, because large wounds are quicker to heal during this period. Treat larger cuts with wound sealant in order to encourage fast healing.

In spring the shoots on a young plant are cut back once they are 20cm (8in) long. Cut back as far as the desired shape will allow. At the same time you can also cut the largest of the remaining leaves.

The next new shoots can be cut back when they reach 10cm (4in) long.

Depending on the size of the tree, older, well-developed plants, can have the first shoots cut back when they reach a length of 5–10cm (2–4in).

A healthy plant will respond quickly and willingly to leaf-cutting by producing new branches, not only where leaves have been removed, but leaf size is not always reduced. The leaves that appear are small at first but they continue to grow. Since the distance between the leaves in dense crowns is relatively large, you can usually leave only one to two leaves the second time you cut them back. Branching thus increases slowly and mainly through the appearance of buds further down the stem.

Wiring

Branches up to the thickness of a pencil can be wired but stronger branches are brought into shape by anchoring. Younger plants grow fast so you should check the wires regularly during the growing period. Wires attached in the spring are usually too tight by midsummer and should be renewed.

Propagation

Fruits ripen in late summer and are collected from the ground, kept over the winter in damp sand in the fridge and sown in spring. Many germinate in the second year.

Saplings should be pruned for the first time in their second year at the very earliest. For the first three to four years, the hazel is best kept in the open ground, or in a container that is bigger than one generally used for bonsai, and cut back regularly. This will result in stronger thickening.

Young plants are usually only found in nurseries but rarely in specialist bonsai nurseries. Pre-shaped saplings or bonsai are also rare. In the wild you will only find plants suitable for bonsai in meadows.

Pests

Spider mites cause a yellowy spotting on the leaves, which later dry up and drop. Control the mites with a pesticide for spider mites (ask in a garden centre).

The bud gall mite (*Phytoptus avellanae*) makes the shrub produce much larger buds. You can control it by removing and destroying the affected parts.

Left: **Hazel leaf and fruit**

Hawthorn

(Crataegus monogyna and Crataegus laevigata)

Both of these species are native trees. They are very similar and only easy to distinguish through their flowers and fruit. The flowers of *Crataegus monogyna* are white, have one style and hairy stems. They are produced about two weeks later than those of *Crataegus laevigata*, which are white with two or even three styles and bald stems. Dark red fruit about 10mm (½in) long develop after pollination by insects, and contain, depending on the number of styles, one to three seeds.

Both plants grow as trees or shrubs; the single-styled type is stronger. The dark green leaves are oval usually with three to five lobes. In the autumn they turn from yellow to orange.

The trunk of the single-styled hawthorn is not uniformly round, and it may have multiple inner stems. The bark flakes off in flat pieces and is dark brown. The branches have numerous thorns on them and shoots that start as thorns.

Both species are common on the edges of woods, in hedgerows, or in the open. They are often planted in gardens, churchyards and parks and are a favourite nesting place for many types of bird.

As bonsai

Far right: **Common hawthorn in autumn, around 20cm (8in) high and ten years old, cultivated from a wild seedling**

The hawthorn likes a sunny to partially shaded position, which may also be very windy. The plant can be kept constantly moist or moderately damp. It is sensitive to lime, so if you use tap water you will need to water constantly to avoid minerals building up in the soil.

The soil can vary greatly. Good results are achieved with, for instance, a mix of loam, sand and peat in equal proportions (1:1:1) by weight. It should be porous, not too fine-grained, and should be renewed every two to three years when the roots should also be pruned.

The hawthorn has a relatively high food requirement so provide a solid organic bonsai fertiliser every two weeks. From late summer reduce the amount of nitrogen, change to using cactus fertiliser, for example.

Overwinter it with the rootball planted in the garden without its container, or on a balcony in a box filled with peat and sand.

Cultivation

The hawthorn can easily be shaped into all the Japanese and other styles but it puts up a good fight with its numerous thorns. Larger saplings are usually too difficult to cultivate without hurting yourself – have plasters to hand.

Saplings with a good root structure and wild seedlings may be shaped between the appearance of the first shoots in spring and the last month of summer.

Wiring

Branches up to ½cm (¼in) thick can be shaped with wires. Attach wires when the new shoots appear and when there are still no leaves in the way. Thickening is not very strong, so a wire positioned in spring can usually remain on the tree until midsummer and is then renewed.

If the wire has not become too tight by autumn, it can stay on the tree over winter and is then removed when the new shoots appear the next year, replacing it with another wire if necessary.

Pruning

Stronger branches are best removed in the spring in order to encourage the tree to heal as quickly as possible. Even so, it will take several years to seal a wound. Apply a wound sealant to all the cuts on the trunk as soon as they have been made.

The hawthorn does not produce long new shoots from all buds in the spring; most of them stop growing after the first leaves have developed. The main shoots on young plants can be cut back to two to five leaves when they are about 15cm (6in) long, depending on how long you want the branch to be. Older plants are cut back earlier to get as fine a twig structure as possible.

Unlike other deciduous trees it is often the bud that is second nearest to the end of the branch that grows after pruning, rather than the one at the end. This means that it is sometimes difficult to direct growth by pruning.

Propagation

Collect seeds in early autumn, remove the flesh of the fruit and keep the seeds in damp sand in the fridge. Sow them in the spring.

Young plants should be readily found near your home or even in your own garden, especially near where birds sit such as by a fence.

Collecting older plants from the wild is only successful in the spring. The tree usually has to develop all its hair roots again, so it is best to remove large sections of the branches directly before or after digging up, in order to avoid too much evaporation when the shoots apear. The tree should then be planted for at least a year in the garden or in a large container, to regenerate.

Young and older cultivated plants are not uncommon in specialist bonsai nurseries.

Hawthorn is often not stocked by many tree nurseries because of its susceptibility to fireblight.

Pests

An attack of spider mites can be recognised by the yellowy dots on the leaves left behind by the sap-sucking insects. Control an attack with a spider mite spray.

Leaf flea (*Psylla crataegi*) makes the leaves wrinkle and they become transparent at the point where the sap was sucked. Hawthorn aphids suck on the branches and cause cancerous growths. They produce whitish, fluffy secretions under which they live. Both pests can be treated with a contact spray such as malathion.

The gall mite (*Dasyneura crataegi*) is recognised by small, pencil-shaped, reddish-green growths on the leaves. It usually makes the new shoots short between the nodes, so that the leaves are squashed together in bunches. The caterpillars of the small frost moth eat the leaves one by one; silkworm moth caterpillars eat in groups at a single leaf. These are all controlled on bonsai by removing them from the tree.

The caterpillars of various spider moths result in defoliation. They produce conspicuous nests and are also controlled by removal from the tree.

Fungal diseases

Mildew is characterised by a white floury covering on the top of the leaves, which then turn brown and drop off. Try to control a single appearance by removing and destroying the affected leaves. If this does not work, or it is a bad case, the plant should be treated several times with a suitable spray, such as benomyl or dinocap. Prevent its occurrence by spraying the plant in the spring when the first shoots appear.

Hawthorn juniper rust makes orangey-yellow blisters which burst open, releasing a yellow powder. It occurs on the underside of the leaves, the leaf stems and the fruit. The fungus also lives on juniper. This condition is quite rare, but, if necessary, control it by spraying several times with a rust fungus spray.

Small brownish spots on the leaves are caused by leaf spot, which can be treated with a suitable spray, such as benomyl.

Bacterial diseases

The hawthorn is very susceptible to fireblight. This is a bacterial disease which makes the tips of the shoots wilt and turn black and can result in whole shoots dying. The black leaves hang from the wilted tips of the shoots. In some areas fireblight is a notifiable disease and must be reported.

Far left: Hawthorn in summer

Below: Hawthorn fruit

Spindle
(Euonymus europaeus)

The spindle, which most commonly occurs as a shrub, occasionally grows to a tree up to 6m (20ft) high. In the wild it can be found in mixed woods, in meadows and on the edge of woods. It is often cultivated in mixed hedgerows.

The alternate leaves appear very early, and turn orange to dark red in early autumn.

The hermaphrodite, inconspicuous greeny-yellow flowers appear in late spring. They are pollinated by insects and develop usually red fruit in a lobed case that resembles a priest's biretta. When ripe they open displaying four seeds surrounded by an orange covering that is lightly attached to the case.

The young branches often have four edges and strips of cork. The trunk forms a finely-fissured, rough, greyish-beige bark.

Right: **Spindle fruit**

Far right: **Spindle in summer, around 40cm (16in) high and twelve years old, cultivated from a bonsai sapling**

As bonsai

Choose a sunny to semi-shaded position that is not protected from the wind. The spindle also tolerates great heat.

The rootball can be kept moist and you can give it hard tap water, as it is classified as lime-loving. But at the same time, it is sensitive to salt so ensure that the water can drain away easily, and always water it so well that any mineral salts that have built up will get washed away.

You can use loam granules (Akadama) alone as a growing medium but mixtures with a high loam content are also acceptable. Young plants need their thick and felty rootball reduced by a third in spring every year before the shoots appear, and the corresponding amount of soil should be renewed. Older plants can remain in the same soil for up to three years.

Feed generously with solid organic bonsai fertiliser from mid-spring until the last four weeks of summer.

Overwinter it with the rootball planted, without the container, in garden soil in light shade, or on a balcony in a box filled with peat and sand.

Cultivation

The spindle can be shaped into any of the styles if you begin early enough. The upright style is easy to achieve, as are the various multiple-trunk styles.

Wiring

Usually only branches up to two years old can be wired as older ones are no longer elastic enough and break easily, but the direction of growth of these can be altered by anchoring.

Wire the plant between the time when the first shoots appear and midsummer. Wires attached in early spring are usually too tight by early summer so they can be removed and often may not need to be replaced.

Pruning

An older branch that is not growing in the right direction and cannot be corrected by wiring can easily be replaced by a new shoot. Where a large branch is removed, numerous new shoots develop in all directions, those that are not needed should be removed as soon as possible in order to stop the trunk thickening at the wound.

The new shoots in spring on younger plants can be cut back to one to three pairs of leaves when they are about 20cm (8in) long, but the position of the branch in the tree as a whole must be taken into account. Make the cut so that the final pair of leaves is set either side of the branch.

To keep the outer branch network delicate, new shoots on older plants can be reduced even earlier, to one or two pairs.

Spindle tolerates leaf cutting from the beginning of summer and

responds by forming new, relatively thin branches with smaller leaves. With increased branching the size of the leaves becomes smaller even without leaf cutting.

Propagation

In some cases the spindle is a protected species and should not be taken from the wild, even as a seed so you can only use cultivated or bought plants as a source. Collect seeds in early autumn, remove the covering and keep them in damp sand in the fridge. Sow them in the spring.

Young plants and older cultivated plants are sometimes found in tree nurseries. Even pre-shaped spindle bonsai are available now and again.

Pests

The black bean aphid (*Aphis fabae*) appears in great numbers very early in the year to suck sap from the new shoots. It causes stunted growth and ruffled leaves. Control it with a low-persistence contact insecticide, such as malathion, or a systemic insecticide.

The numerous greeny-yellow,

Top: European spindle, roughly shaped in the spring

Below left: Spindle flowers

Below right: An attack of spindle spider mite larvae

Far left: Spindle in winter with fruit cases, around 40cm (16in) high and twelve years old, cultivated from a bonsai sapling

black-marked caterpillars of the spindle spider mite (*Yponomeuta evonymellus*) can eat the whole plant bare, and even eat the bark of one-year-old shoots. Control early on by collecting and destroying the caterpillars.

Fungal diseases

Mildew which specialises on *Euonymous* species (*Microsphaera euonymi*) leaves a whitish to dirty-yellow covering on both sides of the leaves. Control a single appearance by removing and destroying affected leaves; a bad case should be treated several times with a spray, such as

benomyl or dinocap. You can prevent an outbreak at the spore stage by using the same spray in the spring while the shoots are appearing.

Blackthorn/Sloe

(Prunus spinosa)

Blackthorn often develops thickets up to 3m (10ft) high, as it spreads easily using root runners. In the wild it is often found on the edge of woods, on the side of hills or on rocky outcrops.

The numerous double-styled white flowers appear before the leaves in mid-spring and make a striking contrast with the black wood of the shrub. After pollination by insects they develop into a fruit like a plum, about 15mm (½in) across, known as a sloe and it is very acid.

The small alternate leaves, in varying shapes, are dark green on top in the summer and usually somewhat duller on the underside, and turning yellow to orange in autumn.

As bonsai

As bonsai the sloe likes a bright, sunny position, but can also be kept in partial shade, tolerating a windy position as well.

Keep it moderately damp, allowing the soil surface to dry off in between watering. It can be watered with hard tap water – blackthorns are not sensitive to mineral salts.

You can use a mix of loam, sand and peat as a growing medium, in proportions of 1:1:1 by weight. The soil is changed every two to three years in the spring, after the flowers and shortly before the shoots. Prune the roots at the same time.

Right: **Sloes**

Feed it generously with organic

bonsai fertiliser from mid-spring to the end of summer.

Overwinter it by planting the rootball without the container in the garden, or on a balcony in a box filled with peat and sand.

Cultivation

The plant's natural habit, as with all shrubs, is not a relevant inspiration for a bonsai. The blackthorn can be cultivated in all the Japanese and other forms. Even when old they do not have particularly thick trunks, and so a height of 50cm (20in) maximum should be planned.

Wiring

Branches up to three years old are relatively easy to wire. Older branches are no longer elastic, but can sometimes be corrected by anchoring. Thickening is limited, so the wire can remain on the plant

for at least a complete growth cycle. In the spring the wire should be examined and, if necessary, removed and replaced with a new one.

Pruning

Older branches should be removed in spring after the blossom has disappeared. Masses of new shoots will develop on large wounds: remove all but one.

In spring new shoots on younger plants are cut back to one to five leaves when they are about 20cm (8in) long, depending on the position of the branch in the tree. To encourage thickening, leave each shoot to grow as long as possible before it is cut back hard.

Older plants can also be cut back to one to two leaves when they are about 10cm (4in) long. Whether one or two leaves remain depends on the desired direction of growth.

Blackthorn responds well to leaf-cutting although it is not really necessary as the blackthorn easily develops a fine twig structure with increasingly smaller leaves.

Propagation

Collect seeds in the autumn after the first frost, remove the flesh of the fruit and keep the seeds in damp sand in the fridge. Sow them in the spring.

Young plants and pre-shaped older plants are sometimes found in specialist bonsai nurseries but you can rarely buy blackthorn bonsai that have been pre-shaped.

Older blackthorn growing in the wild can only be dug up in the spring and then with great effort. The long roots only branch out very deep in the soil, so that only plants with accordingly large rootballs retain fine roots. Cut the branches back when digging it up.

Pests

Small yellowy spots on the leaves, usually followed by malformation, are caused by the gall mite. It is controlled by removing and destroying the affected part of the plant.

The fruit tree spider mite (*Panonychus ulmi*) makes yellowy dots on the leaves which, in a continuing attack, turn grey-green to brown and then drop off. Control it with a spray such as benomyl or dinocap.

Various aphids, often in huge numbers, sometimes make the leaf edges roll up. They can often be washed off with a strong jet of water and in bad cases you can also use a suitable aphid spray.

The slug-like larvae of the black cherry leaf wasp (*Eriocampoides limacina*) eat holes into the top of the leaf leaving only the tissue structure which soon turns dirty grey. You can control it by removing and destroying the affected leaves.

The San Jose scale insect (*Quadraspidiotus perniciosus*), a scale insect that occurs in huge numbers and likes heat, leaves greyish and black patches on the branches. It is quite rare and can be removed quite easily with a toothbrush after which the plant should be treated with a scale insect spray.

The larvae of spider moths can be recognised by their conspicuous nests. They can easily eat a blackthorn bonsai bare in a single attack and should be gathered and destroyed as soon as possible.

Fungal diseases

Plum rust, which changes hosts, is characterised by yellow patches on the underside of the leaf, which later turn into brownish-black blisters. Affected leaves can be removed and destroyed. In a bad case, spray several times with a fungicide such as zineb.

Spray patch disease makes delicate red to brown dots on the leaves, which soon fall from the tree. Control it with the same fungicide that is used for rust fungus.

Blackthorn/ Sloe

Below: **Blackthorn in late summer, around 30cm (1ft) high.** *Designer: Hermann Pieper*

137

Willow

(Salix spp.)

Willows form the largest group of native trees. They prefer damp situations and direct sunlight. This makes them difficult for cultivating as bonsai and they are not really suitable either because of their large leaves, which cannot be reduced in size.

Because there are so many species and as they are not very important for bonsai all willows are dealt with here together and specific varieties are only used as examples if they have special requirements in cultivation.

Most willows, including the sallow, the grey willow, the purple osier and the almond willow, grow as shrubs. Some, such as the silver willow or the marsh willow, develop into magnificent trees. They all have alternate leaves which are different in shape but always undivided.

Willows have separate male and female plants; they are dioecian. The flowers cluster together in yellow catkins with one or two scale-like honey glands; in the male form they have two or, in rare cases, three stamens. They are pollinated by insects and produce wind-borne fruit.

In the wild willows are found in damp, light places, sometimes in small clusters.

Far right: **Golden weeping willow (*Salix alba* 'Chrysocoma'), is a hybrid between the native white willow (*Salix alba*) and the Chinese weeping willow (*Salix babylonica*). This specimen is 80cm (32in) high and is cultivated from a nursery tree.** *Designer: Franz-Josef Thönnessen*

As bonsai

Willows kept as bonsai like a sunny to partially shaded position, which should only be slightly protected from the wind. They have no particular demands as far as water quality goes as long as they receive sufficient. They do need a lot of water and should never be left to dry out. Although most can survive a short period of dryness, they will drop a large number of leaves so give them generous quantities of water, several times on hot days. If this is not possible then put the plant on a tray of rough gravel or hydro pellets which should then be kept constantly full of water. Roots will grow into the tray through the drainage holes in the bonsai container, so water supplies will last longer and can be taken up by the plant from the tray.

It has no particular soil needs although the growing medium should not compact easily because of the amount of watering. A suitable mixture would be loam granules (*Akadama*), sand and peat in proportions of 1:2:1. The soil is changed every two to three years at the same time as the roots are pruned. Spring is the best time for this, before the first leaves appear.

Willows can be fed generously – that is, every two weeks or more often – while they are in the development stage using an organic bonsai fertiliser or mineral fertiliser. After plants have been shaped the nitrogen content should be reduced but the feeding should still be generous.

The first shoots should only be pruned when they have started to harden. Always ensure that your tools are clean as willows are particularly susceptible to fungal diseases.

Although very hardy in the wild, as bonsai willows should be overwintered carefully. Either plant the rootball, without the container, in the earth, or overwinter it in a box filled with peat and sand.

Cultivation

Weeping willows and white willows have a particularly striking natural habit. It is easy to follow their styles in bonsai cultivation but avoid forms where every individual branch is important, such as the upright form, because whole branches often die off. The broom style is also suitable.

Wiring

Willows are easy to wire and even older branches may be bent. Because of the strong thickening growth in willow tree species, the wires should be checked every two weeks.

Branches of a weeping willow only start to 'weep' when they are 1m (3ft) long. The branches are always shorter than this on a bonsai, so the new shoots should be wired downwards as soon as they are strong enough.

Pruning

The first shaping of a sapling should be undertaken during the growing season, at the earliest when the buds begin to appear. During this time larger wounds will heal fast.

Cut back the shoots of younger plants only once a year, in early summer, when they begin to harden. Older willows with well-developed, strong branches, can be cut back more often, when the shoots are about 10cm (4in) long.

Propagation

Due to their tendency to hybridize, and because of the slow growth of seedlings in the first few years, growing willows from seed is not recommended.

Cuttings up to the thickness of your forearm and taken from trees in spring, before the shoots appear, produce roots equally well in water or damp sand. But if they are placed in sand they should not be transferred to another growing medium until the following spring.

Young plants or saplings are rarely found in specialist bonsai nurseries, even though they are easily propagated. In other nurseries there are many sorts, particularly the species that grow as shrubs. Willow bonsai that have already been shaped are hardly ever found in nurseries.

Pests

Gall wasps (*Pontania viminalis*) make reddish-green, round galls, about 1cm (½in) across. Control them by collecting the affected leaves.

Willow leaf beetles and their larvae eat the leaves, often leaving only the veins behind. They can be gathered and then destroyed.

Weevils eat either the buds or the wood and cause stunted shoots or whole parts of the branches to die off. You can control them by collecting the beetles and then removing and destroying the affected parts of the plant. Treat a bad case with a suitable spray.

The willow gall mite causes extensive swelling of parts of the bark. It eventually loosens the bark and reveals holes eaten away in the wood. To control this, remove and destroy affected parts.

The willow scale insect drains the sap under a light green dome, shaped like a mussel shell. You can control it by stripping out the insects or by spraying them with a scale insect spray.

The larvae of the willow cuckoo spit aphid suck on the bark of young branches and protect themselves with a foamy secretion. They can easily be picked off the tree.

Fungal diseases

Mildew produces a white, floury covering on the top and underside of the leaves. Prevent it by using an appropriate spray before the buds burst. Collect and destroy affected leaves.

Willow scab causes distinct brownish-green patches on the leaves and the bark. Affected leaves are dropped prematurely and the tips of shoots die off. Prevent this by using a scab fungus treatment when the first new shoots appear. Affected parts of the plant are removed and destroyed.

Willow rust causes yellow powdery or brownish blisters under the leaves. Affected leaves are dropped prematurely. Control is preventive spraying several times from early summer onwards, and, in the case of an attack, with a rust fungus treatment, such as Bordeaux mixture.

Black canker causes dark brown patches on the leaves and the tips of the shoots turn black and die. To control this use the same treatment as that for willow scab.

Far left: **Crack willow (Salix fragilis) shortly after the first shaping, around 90cm (3ft) high, cultivated from a wild specimen. Designer: Joachim Armbruster**

Below: **Male flowers of the white willow (Salix alba)**

Index

Page numbers in **bold** show where individual species are described in detail.
Page numbers in *italics* show illustrations.